W9-AGD-524

E/NL.1990/Index

COMMISSION ON NARCOTIC DRUGS

ECONOMIC AND SOCIAL COUNCIL

CUMULATIVE INDEX 1987-1990

National Laws and Regulations relating to the Control of Narcotic Drugs and Psychotropic Substances

UNITED NATIONS

NEW YORK, 1991

NOTE

The designations employed and the presentation of material in this publication do not imply the expression of any opinion whatsoever on the part of the Secretariat of the United Nations concerning the legal status of any country, territory, city or area or of its authorities, or concerning the delimitation of its frontiers or boundaries.

E/NL.1990/Index

UNITED NATIONS PUBLICATION

Sales No. E.91.XI.5

ISBN 92-1-148087-6

INTRODUCTION

Purpose of the index

1.   The E/NL. document series of published laws and regulations concerning
narcotic drugs and psychotropic substances is issued on a continuing basis, as
information from Governments is received by the United Nations International
Drug Control Programme. In order to make that information accessible in
convenient form for parliamentary drafters, general research and reference
purposes, cumulative indexes have been designed as companion documents to the
laws and regulations issued in the E/NL. series. To date, cumulative indexes
have been issued for the periods 1947-1965 (E/NL.1965/Index), 1966-1971
(E/NL.1971/Index), 1972-1979 (E/NL.1979/Index) and 1980-1986 (E/NL.1986/Index).

2.   At its first session in 1946, the Commission on Narcotic Drugs observed
that several articles of the conventions pertaining to narcotic drugs 1/
required parties to those conventions to communicate laws and regulations on
narcotic drugs to one another through the good offices of the Secretary-
General. The E/NL. series was established in response to a request by the
Commission to facilitate compliance with that obligation. The same series now
covers the similar requirements for exchange of legislation created by the
more recent international treaties on narcotic drugs and psychotropic
substances. 2/ The United Nations Convention against Illicit Traffic in
Narcotic Drugs and Psychotropic Substances, adopted on 19 December 1988, also
establishes similar requirements, both with respect to legislation concerning
confiscation and general legislation promulgated to give effect to the
Convention. 3/

3.   In practice, laws and regulations are also communicated to the
Secretary-General by States which are not parties to the various conventions.
The texts of the laws and regulations received by the Secretary-General are
edited in standard format, reproduced and distributed to States parties,
non-parties and interested institutions, inter alia, 157 depository libraries
in 55 countries, and members of the public.

4.   The cumulative index was designed both as a comprehensive reference to
the various aspects of drug control laws and regulations and as a practical
tool for use at both the national and international levels, as it provides a
method for continuous mutual disclosure by parties (and non-parties on a
voluntary basis) of their legislative positions in relation to the control
activities required under those conventions.

Contents of the index

5.   This issue of the index covers all national laws and regulations on
narcotic drugs and psychotropic substances which Governments have communicated
to the Secretariat with respect to the period 1987-1990 and which have been
published in the E/NL. series of documents.

6.   The index is divided into five parts, as follows:

(a) Part I

     List of E/NL. documents for the 1987-1990 period in consecutive numerical order, with an indication of the States or territories concerned and the titles of the published laws or regulations;

(b) Part II

     Alphabetical list of States and territories whose laws and regulations have been published in the E/NL. series in the period under consideration, with an indication of the document symbol;

(c) Part III

     Alphabetical list of States and territories appearing in Part II, with an indication of the subjects or control activities covered in the published laws and regulations, followed by the relevant document symbol;

(d) Part IV

     Alphabetical list of the subjects or control activities covered in the laws and regulations, cross-referenced to the States and territories appearing in Part III.

(e) Part V

     Thematic list of the subjects or control activities appearing in Part IV.

Notes

1/   1912 International Opium Convention, article 21; 1925 Agreement concerning the Manufacture of, Internal Trade in, and Use of Prepared Opium, article 30; 1931 Convention for Limiting the Manufacture and Regulating the Distribution of Narcotic Drugs, article 21; 1936 Convention for the Suppression of the Illicit Traffic in Dangerous Drugs, article 16.

2/   Single Convention on Narcotic Drugs, 1961, and that Convention as amended by the 1972 Protocol, article 18; 1971 Convention on Psychotropic Substances, article 16.

3/   United Nations Convention against Illicit Traffic in Narcotic Drugs and Psychotropic Substances, article 5, subparagraph 4(e), and article 20, subparagraph 1(a).

PART I

1987

Philippines - E/NL.1987/1-7 (E)*

E/NL.1987/1   Board Regulation No. 1 s. 1987. Amendment of Board Regulation No. 2-A, Series of 1985, prescribing uniform conditions/requirements for exempted pharmaceutical preparations containing any of the Benzodiazepine substances.

E/NL.1987/2   Board Regulation No. 3 s. 1987, 19 March 1987. Exempting pharmaceutical preparations containing Phenobarbital substances from certain requirements of RA 6425, as amended.

E/NL.1987/3   Board Regulation No. 4 s. 1987, 26 March 1987. Inclusion of Cathinone, Levamphetamine, Levomethamphetamine, Cathine, N-Ethylamphetamine, Fenproporex, Mefenorex, Propylhexedrine and Pyrovalerone in the list of Dangerous Drugs.

E/NL.1987/4   Board Regulation No. 4-A s. 1987, 26 March 1987. Inclusion of DMA, PMA, TMA, DOET, MMDA and MDMA in the list of Dangerous Drugs.

E/NL.1987/5   Board Regulation No. 4-B s. 1987, 26 March 1987. Inclusion of Secbutabarbital and Vinylbital in the list of Dangerous Drugs.

E/NL.1987/6   Board Regulation No. 5 s. 1987, 25 September 1987. Classification of Cathinone as a prohibited drug.

E/NL.1987/7   Board Regulation No. 6 s. 1987, 28 September 1987. Inclusion of Alpha-Methylfentanyl, Acetyl-Alpha-Methylfentanyl, 3-Methylfentanyl, PEPAP, MPPP, in the list of Dangerous Drugs.

Mauritius - E/NL.1987/8 (E)

E/NL.1987/8   The Dangerous Drugs Act, No. 32 of 1986.

Tunisie - E/NL.1987/9 (F)

E/NL.1987/9   Décret No. 86-3 du 7 janvier 1986, fixant les attributions et l'organisation du bureau national des stupéfiants.

---

*E = English
 F = French
 S = Spanish

The titles included in the present list are in the language(s) in which the corresponding laws and regulations have been published: either English only, or French only, or, if the original was in Spanish, in Spanish and English, or Spanish and French.

Turks and Caicos Islands - E/NL.1987/10-11 (E)

E/NL.1987/10   The Narcotic Drugs (Evidence) (United States of America) Ordinance, 1986. No.1 of 1986.

E/NL.1987/11   The Narcotic Drugs (Evidence) (United States of America) (Amendment) Ordinance, 1986. No.6 of 1986.

Guinée-Bissau - E/NL.1987/12 (F)

E/NL.1987/12   Décret Loi No. 1/76. Enumère les peines qui seront infligées aux individus qui violeront les réglements de l'administration publique en ce qui concerne les substances et les plantes classées comme stupéfiants.

China - E/NL.1987/13 (E)

E/NL.1987/13   The Drug Administration Law of the People's Republic of China. September 20, 1984.

United States of America - E/NL.1987/14 (E)

E/NL.1987/14   Controlled Substances Act and Controlled Substances Import and Export Act. Title 21, Chapter 13.

United Kingdom - E/NL.1987/15-20 (E)

E/NL.1987/15   Dangerous Drugs. The Misuse of Drugs (Northern Ireland) Regulations 1986.

E/NL.1987/16   Dangerous Drugs. The Misuse of Drugs (Safe Custody) (Amendment) (Northern Ireland) Regulations 1986.

E/NL.1987/17   Dangerous Drugs. The Misuse of Drugs Act 1971 (Modification) Order 1986.

E/NL.1987/18   Dangerous Drugs. The Misuse of Drugs (Designation) Order 1986.

E/NL.1987/19   Dangerous Drugs. The Misuse of Drugs (Amendment) Regulations 1986.

E/NL.1987/20   Dangerous Drugs. The Misuse of Drugs (Safe Custody) (Amendment) Regulations 1986.

Territoire de la Polynésie Française - E/NL.1987/21-23 (F)

E/NL.1987/21   Arrêté No. 0674 du 1er juillet 1986 portant inscriptions au Tableau B des substances vénéneuses.

E/NL.1987/22   Arrêté No. 1043 du 28 août 1986 portant inscription au Tableau B des substances vénéneuses.

E/NL.1987/23   Arrêté No. 1320 du 28 octobre 1986 édictant certaines prescriptions particulières à l'importation et à la vente au public du trichloréthylène pour usage domestique.

E/NL.1987/24   Orden de 30 de abril de 1986 por la que se establecen los criterios generales de normalización de recetas médicas.

E/NL.1987/25   Orden de 30 de mayo de 1986 por la que se incluyen determinados principios activos en las listas anexas al Convenio de Sustancias Psicotrópicas, hecho en Viena el 21 de febrero de 1971 ratificado por España.

E/NL.1987/26   Real decreto 1418/1986, de 13 de junio, sobre funciones de Ministerio de Sanidad y Consumo en materia de sanidad exterior.

Spain – E/NL.1987/24-26 (E)

E/NL.1987/24   Order of 30 April 1986 establishing the general rules for the standardization of medical prescriptions.

E/NL.1987/25   Order of 30 May 1986 to include specified active substances in the Schedules attached to the Convention on Psychotropic Substances, done in Vienna on 21 February 1971 and ratified by Spain.

E/NL.1987/26   Royal Decree No. 1418 of 13 June 1986 regarding the functions of the Ministry of Health and Consumer Affairs in the area of external health.

Hongrie – E/NL.1987/27-28 (F)

E/NL.1987/27   Arrêté conjoint du Ministre de la santé et du Ministre de l'intérieur No. 4/1986 (VIII.10).

E/NL.1987/28   Arrêté du Ministre de la santé No. 11/1986 (X.2).

Italie – E/NL.1987/29 (F)

E/NL.1987/29   Loi No. 663 du 19 Octobre 1986. Article 12 amendant l'article 47 bis de la loi No. 354 du 26 juillet 1974, concernant la mesure alternative de remise au service social avec mise à l'épreuve.

Argentina – E/NL.1987/30-36 (S)

E/NL.1987/30   Decreto del Poder Ejecutivo Nacional del 13 de marzo de 1986.

E/NL.1987/31   Resolución del Ministerio de Salud y Acción Social No. 682 del 21 de agosto de 1986.

E/NL.1987/32   Ley No. 23.358 del 27 de agosto de 1986.

E/NL.1987/33   Resolución del Ministerio de Salud y Acción Social No. 977 del 17 de noviembre de 1986.

E/NL.1987/34   Resolución del Ministerio de Salud y Acción Social No. 1031 del 9 de diciembre de 1986.

E/NL.1987/35   Resolución del Ministerio de Salud y Acción Social No. 1435 del 19 de diciembre de 1986.

E/NL.1987/36   Resolución de la Administración Nacional de Aduanas No. 0751
del 3 de abril de 1987.

Argentine - E/NL.1987/30-36 (F)

E/NL.1987/30   Décret du pouvoir exécutif national, en date du 13 mars 1986.

E/NL.1987/31   Arrêté No. 682 du Ministère de la santé et des affaires
sociales, en date du 21 août 1986.

E/NL.1987/32   Loi No. 23.358, en date du 27 août 1986.

E/NL.1987/33   Arrêté No. 997 du Ministère de la santé et des affaires
sociales, en date du 17 novembre 1986.

E/NL.1987/34   Arrêté No. 1031 du Ministère de la santé et des affaires
sociales, en date du 9 décembre 1986.

E/NL.1987/35   Arrêté No. 1435 du Ministère de la santé et des affaires
sociales, en date du 19 décembre 1986.

E/NL.1987/36   Arrêté No. 0751 de l'Administration nationale des douanes, en
date du 3 avril 1987.

Austria - E/NL.1987/37-38 (E)

E/NL.1987/37   Narcotic Drugs Act, 1951, as amended by the Narcotic Drugs
Amendment Act, 1971, the Penal Code Adaptation Act and the
Narcotic Drugs Amendment Acts, 1977, 1980 and 1985.

E/NL.1987/38   Order by Federal Minister of Health and the Environment of 18
December 1986 amending the Narcotic Drugs Order 1979 (Narcotic
Drugs Order Amendment 1986).

Costa Rica - E/NL.1987/39 (S)

E/NL.1987/39   Reglamento No. 17165-S de importación de precursores,
productos químicos y disolventes.

Costa Rica - E/NL.1987/39 (E)

E/NL.1987/39   Regulation No. 17165-S governing the import of precursor
chemicals and solvents.

Singapore - E/NL.1987/40-41 (E)

E/NL.1987/40   The Poisons Act (Chapter 164), The Poisons (Amendment) Rules
1986.

E/NL.1987/41   The Poisons Act (Chapter 164), The Poisons Act (Amendment of
Schedule), Notification 1986.

Hong Kong - E/NL.1987/42-43 (E)

E/NL.1987/42   Drug Addicts Treatment and Rehabilitation (Amendment)
Ordinance 1986, No. 28/86.

E/NL.1987/43   Pharmacy and Poisons (Amendment) Ordinance 1986, No. 58/86.

<u>Cayman Islands – E/NL.1987/44 (E)</u>

E/NL.1987/44   The Misuse of Drugs (Amendment) Law, 1987 (Law 12 of 1987).

<u>India – E/NL.1987/45 (E)</u>

E/NL.1987/45   Order of 17 March 1986 constituting the "Narcotics Control Bureau".

<u>Cyprus – E/NL.1987/46 (E)</u>

E/NL.1987/46   The Narcotic Drugs and Psychotropic Substances (Amendment) Regulations, 1986.

<u>Belgique – E/NL.1987/47–48 (F)</u>

E/NL.1987/47   Arrêté royal du 31 octobre 1985, modifiant l'arrêté royal du 31 décembre 1930 concernant le trafic des substances soporifiques et stupéfiantes.

E/NL.1987/48   Arrêté royal du 26 septembre 1986, modifiant l'arrêté royal du 31 mai 1976 réglementant certains psychotropes.

<u>France – E/NL.1987/49–56 (F)</u>

E/NL.1987/49   Arrêté du 17 décembre 1984 portant modifications aux exonérations, en médecine humaine, de la réglementation des substances vénéneuses.

E/NL.1987/50   Arrêté du 31 janvier 1985. Modification aux tableaux des substances vénéneuses (section II).

E/NL.1987/51   Décret No. 85.191 du 7 février 1985 modifiant le décret No. 82.10 du 8 janvier 1982 portant création du Comité interministériel de lutte contre la toxicomanie et de la Mission permanente de lutte contre la toxicomanie.

E/NL.1987/52   Arrêté du 26 mars 1985 portant inscription aux tableaux des substances vénéneuses (section II).

E/NL.1987/53   Décret No. 86.1327 du 10 décembre 1985.

E/NL.1987/54   Loi No. 86.76 du 17 janvier 1986 portant diverses dispositions d'ordre social.

E/NL.1987/55   Arrêté du 9 juillet 1986 portant inscriptions au tableau des substances vénéneuses (section II).

E/NL.1987/56   Décret No. 86.847 du 18 juillet 1986 modifiant le décret No. 82.10 du 8 janvier 1982 modifié portant création du Comité interministériel et de la Mission interministérielle de lutte contre la toxicomanie.

Luxembourg E/NL.1987/57-61 (F)

E/NL.1987/57   Réglement grand-ducal du 22 août 1985 complétant l'annexe du réglement grand-ducal du 20 mars 1974 concernant certaines substances psychotropes.

E/NL.1987/58   Réglement grand-ducal du 13 décembre 1985 modifiant l'annexe du réglement grand-ducal du 4 mars 1974 concernant certaines substances toxiques.

E/NL.1987/59   Réglement grand-ducal du 13 juin 1986 modifiant l'annexe du réglement grand-ducal du 4 mars 1974 concernant certaines substances toxiques.

E/NL.1987/60   Réglement grand-ducal du 13 juin 1986 complétant l'annexe du réglement grand-ducal du 20 mars 1974 concernant certaines substances psychotropes.

E/NL.1987/61   Réglement grand-ducal du 23 janvier 1987 modifiant le réglement grand-ducal modifié du 26 mars 1974 établissant la liste des stupéfiants.

Qatar - E/NL.1987/62 (E)

E/NL.1987/62   Law No. 9, 1987, to control narcotic drugs and dangerous psychotropic substances and to regulate their use and trade therein.

Paraguay - E/NL.1987/63 (S)

E/NL.1987/63   Ley No. 1.340 que modifica y actualiza la Ley No. 357/72, que reprime el tráfico ilícito de estupefacientes y drogas peligrosas y otros delitos afines y establece medidas de prevención y recuperación de farmacodependientes.

Paraguay - E/NL.1987/63 (E)

E/NL.1987/63   Law No. 1,340 amending and updating Law No. 357/72, which suppresses the illicit traffic in narcotic and dangerous drugs and other associated offences and establishes measures for the prevention of drug addiction and the recovery of drug addicts.

France - E/NL.1987/64-65 (F)

E/NL.1987/64   Décret No. 87-729 du 28 août 1987 relatif aux dissolutions de caoutchouc et aux colles à boyaux.

E/NL.1987/65   Loi No. 87-1157 du 31 décembre 1987 relative à la lutte contre le trafic de stupéfiants et modifiant certaines dispositions du code pénal.

Colombia − E/NL.1987/66-71 (S)

E/NL.1987/66   Decreto No. 3665 del 17 de diciembre de 1986.
Control y tráfico de estupefacientes.

E/NL.1987/67   Decreto No. 3667 del 19 de diciembre de 1986.
Restablecimiento del orden público.

E/NL.1987/68   Decreto No. 3671 del 19 de diciembre de 1986.
Competencia y procedimientos en materia de narcotráfico.

E/NL.1987/69   Decreto No. 3673 del 19 de diciembre de 1986.
Medidas tendientes a combatir la impunidad.

E/NL.1987/70   Decreto No. 3788 del 31 de diciembre de 1986.
Reglamentación de la Ley No. 30 de 1986 o Estatuto Nacional de
Estupefacientes.

E/NL.1987/71   Resolución No. 009 del 18 de febrero de 1987.
Reglamentación de la importación, fabricación, distribución,
transporte y uso de Acetona, Cloroformo, Eter Etílico, Acido
Clorhídrico y demás sustancias a que hace referencia el
literal f) del artículo 20 de la Ley 30 de 1986.

Colombia − E/NL.1987/66-71 (E)

E/NL.1987/66   Decree No. 3665 of 17 December 1986.
Control of narcotic drugs trafficking.

E/NL.1987/67   Decree No. 3667 of 19 December 1986.
Re-establishment of public order.

E/NL.1987/68   Decree No. 3671 of 19 December 1986.
Competence and procedures in respect of drug trafficking.

E/NL.1987/69   Decree No. 3673 of 19 December 1986.
Measures aimed at combating impunity.

E/NL.1987/70   Decree No. 3788 of 31 December 1986.
Regulation of Law No. 30 of 1986 or
National Narcotic Drugs Statute.

E/NL.1987/71   Resolution No. 009 of 18 February 1987.
Regulation of the import, manufacture, distribution, transport
of and use of acetone, chloroform, ethyl ether, hydrochloric
acid and other substances referred to in article 20,
paragraph (f), of Law No. 30 of 1986.

Ecuador − E/NL.1987/72 (S)

E/NL.1987/72   Codificación de la ley de control y fiscalización del tráfico
de estupefacientes y sustancias psicotrópicas, 15 de octubre
de 1986.

Equateur − E/NL.1987/72 (F)

E/NL.1987/72   Codification de la loi sur le contrôle des stupéfiants et des
substances psychotropes et la lutte contre le trafic des
stupéfiants et des substances psychotropes.

<u>Federal Republic of Germany - E/NL.1987/73-74 (E)</u>

E/NL.1987/73   First Ordinance Amending the Regulations of Narcotic Drugs
                Legislation (First Narcotic Drugs Legislation Amending
                Ordinance), 6 August 1984.

E/NL.1987/74   Second Ordinance Amending the Regulations of Narcotic Drugs
                Legislation (Second Narcotic Drugs Legislation Amending
                Ordinance), 23 July 1986.

<u>United Arab Emirates - E/NL.1987/75 (E)</u>

E/NL.1987/75   Federal Law No. 6 of 1986 on the control of narcotic
                substances and like substances.

<u>Oman - E/NL.1987/76-79 (E)</u>

E/NL.1987/76   Circular No. 11/1982 of 10 May 1982.

E/NL.1987/77   Circular No. 18/86 of 29 March 1986.

E/NL.1987/78   Circular No. 27/86 of 27 May 1986.

E/NL.1987/79   Circular No. 21/87 of 6 May 1987.

<u>Venezuela - E/NL.1987/80 (S)</u>

E/NL.1987/80   Resolución Conjunta de los Ministerios de Hacienda No. 255, de
                Fomento No. 2126 y de Justicia No. 18, del 19 de junio de 1985.

<u>Venezuela - E/NL.1987/80 (E)</u>

E/NL.1987/80   Joint Resolution of the Ministry of the Treasury No. 255, the
                Ministry of Public Works No. 2,126 and the Ministry of Justice
                No. 18 of 19 June 1985.

<u>Malta - E/NL.1987/81-87 (E)</u>

E/NL.1987/81   Act No. VIII of 1986. An act further to amend the Dangerous
                Drugs Ordinance, Cap. 161.

E/NL.1987/82   Act No. XVII of 1986. An act further to amend the Medical and
                Kindred Professions Ordinance, Cap. 51.

E/NL.1987/83   Medical and Kindred Professions Ordinance (Cap.51). Drugs
                (Registration of Addicts) Regulations, 1986.

E/NL.1987/84   Medical and Kindred Professions Ordinance (Cap.51).
                Psychotropic Drugs Regulations, 1986.

E/NL.1987/85   Dangerous Drugs Ordinance (Cap. 161). Dangerous Drugs
                (Internal Control) (Amendment) Rules, 1986.

E/NL.1987/86   Medical and Kindred Professions Ordinance (Cap.51). Drugs
                (Control) (Amendment) Regulations, 1986.

E/NL.1987/87   Medical and Kindred Professions Ordinance (Cap.51). Drugs
                (Control) (Amendment) Regulations, 1987.

<u>Syrian Arab Republic - E/NL.1987/88-89 (E)</u>

E/NL.1987/88   Instructions of 13 May 1986 concerning the importation, distribution, prescription and dispensing of psychotropic substances.

E/NL.1987/89   Regulatory decree of 27 July 1986.

1988

<u>Australia - E/NL.1988/1-2 (E)</u>

E/NL.1988/1   Mutual Assistance in Criminal Matters Act, No 85 of 1987.

E/NL.1988/2   Proceeds of Crime Act, No. 87 of 1987.

<u>España - E/NL.1988/3-4 (S)</u>

E/NL.1988/3   Ley orgánica 1/1988, de 24 de marzo, de Reforma del Código Penal en materia de tráfico ilegal de drogas.

E/NL.1988/4   Ley 5/1988, de 24 de marzo, por la que se crea la Fiscalía Especial para la Prevención y Represión del Tráfico Ilegal de Drogas.

<u>Spain - E/NL.1988/3-4 (E)</u>

E/NL.1988/3   Constitutional Law 1/1988, of 24 March, amending the Criminal Code with respect to Illicit Trafficking in Drugs.

E/NL.1988/4   Law 5/1988, of 24 March, establishing the Special Office of the Public Prosecutor for the Prevention and Suppression of Illicit Trafficking in Drugs.

<u>Italy - E/NL.1988/5-9 (E)</u>

E/NL.1988/5   Updated text of Law No. 1423 of 27 December 1956 - Preventive measures in respect of persons posing a danger to security and public morality.

E/NL.1988/6   Updated text of Law No. 575 of 31 May 1965 - Provisions against the mafia.

E/NL.1988/7   Excerpts of Law No. 152 of 22 May 1975 - Provisions for the protection of public order.

E/NL.1988/8   Excerpts of Law No. 646 of 13 September 1982 - Provisions in the area of preventive measures in respect of assets, and additions to Laws No. 1423 of 27 December 1956, No. 57 of 10 February 1962 and No. 575 of 31 May 1965; establishment of a parliamentary commission on the phenomenon of the mafia.

E/NL.1988/9   Excerpts of Decree-Law No. 629 of 6 September 1982, co-ordinated with Conversion Law No. 726 of 12 October 1982 (Urgent measures for the co-ordination of the campaign against mafia criminality).

Bahamas − E/NL.1988/10-12 (E)

E/NL.1988/10   Chapter 213. Dangerous Drugs. An Act to Regulate the Importation, Exportation, Manufacture, Sale and Use of Opium and Other Dangerous Drugs, as amended. (27 February 1939)

E/NL.1988/11   An Act to make provision for the Tracing of the Proceeds of Drug Trafficking, the Confiscation of those proceeds and ancillary amendments to the Dangerous Drugs Act. (6 January 1987)

E/NL.1988/12   An Act to amend the Dangerous Drugs Act. (27 March 1988)

Sénégal − E/NL.1988/13-15 (F)

E/NL.1988/13   Loi No. 77−109 du 26 décembre 1977 abrogeant et remplaçant l'article 2 et le deuxième alinéa de l'article 3 de la loi No. 72.24 du 19 avril 1972 relative à la répression des infractions en matière de stupéfiants.

E/NL.1988/14   Loi No. 87−12 du 24 février 1987 abrogeant et remplacant les articles 3, 4, 10 et le 4ème paragraphe de l'article 6 de la loi No. 72−24 du 19 avril 1972 relative à la répression des infractions en matière de stupéfiants.

E/NL.1988/15   Décret No. 87−415 du 3 avril 1987 portant création d'une Commission nationale des stupéfiants.

Côte d'Ivoire − E/NL.1988/16-17 (F)

E/NL.1988/16   Décret No. 85−351 du 8 mai 1985 portant modification du Comité ivoirien de lutte contre l'usage abusif des drogues (CILAD).

E/NL.1988/17   Loi No. 88−686 du 22 juillet 1988 portant répression du trafic et de l'usage illicites des stupéfiants, des substances psychotropes et des substances vénéneuses.

Bénin − E/NL.1988/18 (F)

E/NL.1988/18   Loi No. 87−009 du 21 septembre 1987 relative à la répression des infractions en matière d'usage, de commerce, de détention et d'emploi de substances vénéneuses.

France − E/NL.1988/19-20 (F)

E/NL.1988/19   Décret No. 87−328 du 13 mai 1987 portant suspension des dispositions du décret No. 72−200 du 13 mars 1972 réglementant le commerce et l'importation des seringues et des aiguilles destinées aux injections parentérales en vue de lutter contre l'extension de la toxicomanie.

E/NL.1988/20   Décret No. 88−894 du 24 août 1988 portant suspension de dispositions du décret No. 72−200 du 13 mars 1972 réglementant le commerce et l'importation des seringues et des aiguilles destinées aux injections parentérales en vue de lutter contre l'extension de la toxicomanie et modification dudit décret.

España - E/NL.1988/21-24 (S)

E/NL.1988/21   Orden de 6 de octubre de 1987 por la que se incluyen
                determinados principios activos en las listas anexas al
                Convenio de Sustancias Sicotrópicas, hecho en Viena el
                21 de febrero, de 1971, ratificado por España.

E/NL.1988/22   Orden de 14 de enero de 1988 por la que se convocan ayudas
                económicas destinadas a Entidades sin fines de lucro, de
                ámbito estatal, que desarrollen programas supracomunitarios en
                el marco de las prioridades del Plan Nacional sobre Drogas
                para 1988.

E/NL.1988/23   Orden de 20 de diciembre de 1988 por la que se incluyen
                determinados principios activos en las listas I y IV anexas a
                la Convención Unica de 1961 sobre Estupefacientes.

E/NL.1988/24   Orden de 20 de diciembre de 1988 por la que se incluyen
                determinados principios activos en la lista II anexa al
                Convenio de Sustancias Sicotrópicas de 1971.

Spain - E/NL.1988/21-24 (E)

E/NL.1988/21   Order of 6 October 1987 to include specified active substances
                in the Schedules attached to the Convention on Psychotropic
                Substances, done in Vienna on 21 February 1971 and ratified by
                Spain.

E/NL.1988/22   Order of 14 January 1988 providing for financial assistance to
                non-profit-making bodies associated with the State, which are
                carrying out regional programmes in accordance with the
                priorities of the National Drugs Plan for 1988.

E/NL.1988/23   Order of 20 December 1988 to include specified active
                substances in Schedules I and IV attached to the Single
                Convention on Narcotic Drugs, 1961.

E/NL.1988/24   Order of 20 December 1988 to include specified active
                substances in Schedule II attached to the Convention on
                Psychotropic Substances, 1971.

Bolivia - E/NL.1988/25 (S)

E/NL.1988/25   Ley del regimen de la coca y sustancias controladas, No. 1008
                de 19 de julio de 1988.

Bolivia - E/NL.1988/25 (E)

E/NL.1988/25   Law on the Regime Applicable to Coca and Controlled
                Substances, No. 1008 of 19 July 1988.

Belgique - E/NL.1988/26-27 (F)

E/NL.1988/26   Arrêté royal du 20 février 1987 modifiant l'arrêté royal du
                31 décembre 1930 concernant le trafic des substances
                soporifiques et stupéfiantes.

E/NL.1988/27   Arrêté royal du 21 décembre 1988 modifiant l'arrêté royal du 31 décembre 1930 concernant le trafic des substances soporifiques et stupéfiantes.

Malaysia - E/NL.1988/28-31 (E)

E/NL.1988/28   Act 316. Dangerous Drugs (Special Preventive Measures) Act 1985.

E/NL.1988/29   Act A629. Dangerous Drugs (Special Preventive Measures) (Amendment) Act 1985.

E/NL.1988/30   Act A707. Dangerous Drugs (Special Preventive Measures) (Amendment) Act 1988.

E/NL.1988/31   Act 340. Dangerous Drugs (Forfeiture of Property) Act 1988.

Cape Verde - E/NL.1988/32 (E)

E/NL.1988/32   Decree No. 80-A/88. To approve the National Medicines List and to supersede Decree No. 123/80.

Cayman Islands - E/NL.1988/33 (E)

E/NL.1988/33   The Misuse of Drugs (Amendment) Law, 1988.

Trinidad and Tobago - E/NL.1988/34 (E)

E/NL.1988/34   The Food and Drugs (Amendment) Regulations, 1987.

Thailand - E/NL.1988/35-39 (E)

E/NL.1988/35   The Psychotropic Substances Act (No. 2), B.E. 2528 (1985).

E/NL.1988/36   Notification No. 43 of 1986, specifying names and schedules of psychotropic substances which must have warnings and precautions.

E/NL.1988/37   Ministerial Regulation No. 18 of 1987.

E/NL.1988/38   Notification No. 51 of 1988, specifying names and schedules of psychotropic substances as of the Psychotropic Substances Act, 1975.

E/NL.1988/39   Notification No. 53 of 1988, specifying names of psychotropic substances which must have warnings or cautions as of the Psychotropic Substances Act, 1975.

Turkey E/NL.1988/40-41 (E)

E/NL.1988/40   Regulations on the implementation of Article 21 of Law 2313 regarding the Control of Narcotic Drugs.

E/NL.1988/41   Provisions related to Narcotic Drugs in the Turkish Penal Code No. 765 of 1 March 1926, as amended by Law 2275 of 8 August 1933, Law 6123 of 9 July 1953 and Law 2370 of 7 January 1981.

San Marino - E/NL.1988/42 (E)

E/NL.1988/42   Law No. 32 of 7 March 1988. Additions to the Provisions of
the Criminal Code and Code of Criminal Procedure Regarding
Offences Involving Narcotic Substances.

Israel - E/NL.1988/43 (E)

E/NL.1988/43   Drug Control Authority Law, 5748-1988
(14 June 1988).

New Zealand - E/NL.1988/44-45 (E)

E/NL.1988/44   Misuse of Drugs Amendment Act 1987.

E/NL.1988/45   Misuse of Drugs Amendment Act (No. 2) 1987.

Colombia - E/NL.1988/46-48 (S)

E/NL.1988/46   Resolución No. 0010 de 25 de febrero de 1988. Modificación de
la resolución No. 009 de 18 de febrero de 1987.

E/NL.1988/47   Resolución No. 0011 de 25 de febrero de 1988. Autorización a
los Consejos Seccionales de Estupefacientes.

E/NL.1988/48   Resolución No. 0056 de 1º de septiembre de 1988.
Reglamentación de la expedición del certificado de carencia.

Colombia - E/NL.1988/46-48 (E)

E/NL.1988/46   Resolution No. 0010 of 25 February 1988. Amending
Resolution No. 009 of 18 February 1987.

E/NL.1988/47   Resolution No. 0011 of 25 February 1988. Authorization for the
Sectional Narcotic Drugs Councils.

E/NL.1988/48   Resolution No. 0056 of 1 September 1988. Regulating the issue
of the certificate of absence.

Pakistan - E/NL.1988/49 (E)

E/NL.1988/49   Dangerous Drugs Act, 1930 (II of 1930).   Amendment of
section 2 and section 23. Insertion of new chapter IV A.

Chile - E/NL.1988/50-52 (S)

E/NL.1988/50   Decreto No. 752. Modifica Decreto Supremo No. 405 de 1983.
24 de diciembre de 1987.

E/NL.1988/51   Decreto No. 284. Modifica Decreto Supremo No. 405 de 1983.
21 de septiembre de 1988.

E/NL.1988/52   Decreto No. 344. Modifica Decreto No. 67 de 1985.
14 de noviembre de 1988.

Chile - E/NL.1988/50-52 (E)

E/NL.1988/50	Decree No. 752. Amends Supreme Decree No. 405 of 1983. 24 December 1987.
E/NL.1988/51	Decree No. 284. Amends Supreme Decree No. 405 of 1983. 21 September 1988.
E/NL.1988/52	Decree No. 344. Amends Decree No. 67 of 1985. 14 November 1988.

Argentina - E/NL.1988/53-59 (S)

E/NL.1988/53	Resolución No. 129. 6 de febrero de 1987.
E/NL.1988/54	Resolución No. 672. 7 de agosto de 1987.
E/NL.1988/55	Resolución No. 242. 17 de marzo de 1988.
E/NL.1988/56	Decreto No. 528. 26 de abril de 1988.
E/NL.1988/57	Resolución No. 1,008. 21 de noviembre de 1988.
E/NL.1988/58	Orden No. 2,395. 24 de noviembre de 1988.
E/NL.1988/59	Resolución No. 2,622. 2 de diciembre de 1988.

Argentina - E/NL.1988/53-59 (E)

E/NL.1988/53	Resolution No. 129 of 6 February 1987.
E/NL.1988/54	Resolution No. 672 of 7 August 1987.
E/NL.1988/55	Resolution No. 242 of 17 March 1988.
E/NL.1988/56	Decree No. 528 of 26 April 1988.
E/NL.1988/57	Resolution No. 1,008 of 21 November 1988.
E/NL.1988/58	Order No. 2,395 of 24 November 1988.
E/NL.1988/59	Resolution No. 2,622 of 2 December 1988.

Hongrie - E/NL.1988/60-61 (F)

E/NL.1988/60	Arrêté du Ministre de la santé No. 15/1987 (X.15).
E/NL.1988/61	Décret pris en Conseil des Ministres No. 1065/1987 (XII.10).

Sweden - E/NL.1988/62-66 (E)

E/NL.1988/62	Notification on List of Narcotics, 23 January 1987 (SOSFS 1987:2).
E/NL.1988/63	Decree by the National Board of Health and Welfare, 6 May 1987 (SOSFS 1987:10).

E/NL.1988/64   Decree by the National Board of Health and Welfare,
                9 July 1987 (SOSFS 1987:10).

E/NL.1988/65   Ordinance regarding change of the Narcotics Ordinance,
                3 December 1987 (SFS 1987:1081).

E/NL.1988/66   Regulations from the National Board of Health and Welfare on
                methadone maintenance treatment and the prescription of
                opiates for drug addiction, 29 January 1988 (SOSFS 1988:4).

Thailand - E/NL.1988/67-68 (E)

E/NL.1988/67   Narcotics Act (No. 2), B.E. 2528 (1985).

E/NL.1988/68   Narcotics Act (No. 3), B.E. 2530 (1987).

Netherlands Antilles - E/NL.1988/69-72 (E)

E/NL.1988/69   Ministerial Decree of January 22, 1987 pursuant to article 3,
                paragraph 2, article 5, paragraphs 1 and 2, and article 7,
                paragraph 2 of the Opium National Ordinance 1960, containing
                new provisions in regard to the dispensing and prescribing of
                medicines referred to in article 3 and article 4 of the
                aforementioned national ordinance.

E/NL.1988/70   Ministerial Decree of May 22, 1987 to determine the new
                schedule pertaining to the Ministerial Decree of August 27,
                1986, pursuant to article 3, first paragraph sub g, of the
                Opium National Ordinance 1960.

E/NL.1988/71   National Order of January 29, 1988 No. 1, to create the
                National Council concerning Consciousness Altering Drugs.

E/NL.1988/72   Ministerial Decree of August 10, 1988 pursuant to article 3,
                paragraph 1 under g of the Opium National Ordinance 1960.

Roumanie - E/NL.1988/73 (F)

E/NL.1988/73   Ordre du ministère de la santé concernant la modification de
                l'annexe No. 1 aux Instructions No. 103/1970 pour l'exécution
                des spécifications de la loi No. 73/1969 sur le régime des
                produits et des substances stupéfiantes.

Sri Lanka - E/NL.1988/74 (E)

E/NL. 1988/74   Poisons, Opium and Dangerous Drugs (Amendment)
                Act No. 26 of 1986.

Hong Kong - E/NL.1988/75-76 (E)

E/NL.1988/75   Dangerous Drugs (Amendment) Ordinance 1987, No. 24 of 1987.

E/NL.1988/76   Pharmacy and Poisons (Amendment) Regulations 1987, L.N. 85 of
                1987.

France - E/NL.1989/5-8 (F)

E/NL.1989/5   Arrêté du 26 juillet 1988 portant inscription aux tableaux des substances vénéneuses (section II).

E/NL.1989/6   Arrêté du 2 septembre 1988 portant modifications aux tableaux des substances vénéneuses (section II).

E/NL.1989/7   Arrêté du 15 décembre 1988 portant modification des tableaux des substances vénéneuses et des exonérations de la réglementation des substances vénéneuses (section II).

E/NL.1989/8   Décret No. 88.1232 du 29 décembre 1988 relatif aux substances et préparations vénéneuses et modifiant le code de la santé publique (deuxième partie).

India - E/NL.1989/9-10 (E)

E/NL.1989/9   The Prevention of Illicit Traffic in Narcotic Drugs and Psychotropic Substances Act, 1988. (Act No. 46 of 1988).

E/NL.1989/10   The Narcotic Drugs and Psychotropic Substances (Amendment) Act, 1988. (Act No. 2 of 1989).

Belgique - E/NL.1989/11-12 (F)

E/NL.1989/11   Arrêté royal du 11 juin 1987 concernant certaines substances toxiques pouvant être utilisées pour la synthèse de substances stupéfiantes ou psychotropes.

E/NL.1989/12   Arrêté royal du 2 décembre 1988 réglementant certaines substances psychotropes.

Saint Lucia - E/NL.1989/13 (E)

E/NL.1989/13   Drugs (Prevention of Misuse) Act, No. 22 of 1988.

Egypt - E/NL.1989/14 (E)

E/NL.1989/14   Law No. 122 of 1989.   Amending Certain Provisions of Decree-Law No. 182 of 1960 Concerning the Control of Narcotic Drugs and Regulation of their Utilization and Trade.

Thailand- E/NL.1989/15-16 (E)

E/NL.1989/15   Ministerial Regulation B.E. 2528 (1985) on the Storage of the Seized Narcotic Drugs.

E/NL1989/16   Ministerial Regulation B.E. 2532 (1989) on the Storage of the Seized Narcotic Drugs (No. 2).

Argentina - E/NL.1989/17 (S)

E/NL.1989/17   Código Penal. Ley No. 23.737. Su Modificación.

Argentine - E/NL.1989/17 (F)

E/NL.1989/17   Code pénal. Loi No. 23 737. Modification de la loi.

India – E/NL.1989/18-19 (E)

E/NL.1989/18   Section 52A on Disposal of seized narcotic drugs and psychotropic substances, incorporated in December 1988 into the Narcotic Drugs and Psychotropic Substances Act, 1985.

E/NL.1989/19   Standing Order No 1/89.

Uruguay – E/NL.1989/20-21 (S)

E/NL.1989/20   Decreto 593/87 del 6 de octubre de 1987, por lo que se establece que la venta de medicamentos que contengan las sustancias que se determinan deberán ser prescritos en las recetas para estupefacientes del Ministerio de Salud Pública.

E/NL.1989/21   Ley No. 16.034 del 18 abril de 1989.

Uruguay – E/NL.1989/20-21 (F)

E/NL.1989/20   Décret 593/87 du 6 octobre 1987, stipulant que les médicaments contenant les substances indiquées doivent être prescrits sur des ordonnances pour stupéfiants délivrées par le Ministère de la santé publique.

E/NL.1989/21   Loi No. 16.034 du 18 avril 1989.

Costa Rica – E/NL.1989/22 (S)

E/NL.1989/22   Ley No. 7093 sobre Sustancias Psicotrópicas, Drogas de uso no Autorizado y Actividades Conexas.

Costa Rica – E/NL.1989/22 (E)

E/NL.1989/22   Law No. 7093 on Psychotropic Substances, Drugs of unauthorized Use and Related Activities.

Luxembourg – E/NL.1989/23 (F)

E/NL.1989/23   Loi du 7 juillet 1989 portant modification de la loi modificé du 19 février 1973 concernant la vente de substances médicamenteuses et la lutte contre la toxicomanie.

Dominica – E/NL.1989/24 (E)

E/NL.1989/24   Drugs (Prevention of Misuse) Act, No. 20 of 1988.

Zambia – E/NL.1989/25-26 (E)

E/NL.1989/25   The Dangerous Drugs (Forfeiture of Property) Act, 1989.

E/NL.1989/26   The Dangerous Drugs (Forfeiture of Property) (Special Organisations) (Drugs Enforcement Commission) Regulations, 1989.

United States of America – E/NL.1989/27-28 (E)

E/NL.1989/27   Chemical Diversion and Trafficking Act of 1988.
(Anti-Drug Abuse Act of 1988, Title VI, Subtitle A)

E/NL.1989/28   Money Laundering Prosecution Improvement Act of 1988.
(Anti-Drug Abuse Act of 1988, Title VI, Subtitle E)

Hongrie – E/NL.1989/29-30 (F)

E/NL.1989/29   Arrêté du Ministre des affaires sociales
et de la santé N° 12/1988 (X.14).

E/NL.1989/30   Arrêté du Ministre des affaires sociales
et de la santé N° 13/1988 (X.14).

United Kingdom – E/NL.1989/31-32 (E)

E/NL.1989/31   Dangerous Drugs. Misuse of Drugs (Amendment) Regulations 1988.

E/NL.1989/32   Dangerous Drugs. Misuse of Drugs (Amendment) Regulations
(Northern Ireland) 1988.

Polynésie Francaise – E/NL.1989/33 (F)

E/NL.1989/33   Arrêté No. 1134 du 3 octobre 1988 portant inscription au
Tableau B des substances vénéneuses (section II).

Nouvelle-Calédonie et Dépendances – E/NL.1989/34 (F)

E/NL.1989/34   Arrêté No. 3308 du 14 décembre 1988 portant modifications aux
tableaux des substances vénéneuses (section II).

Thailand – E/NL.1989/35-36 (E)

E/NL.1989/35   Notification of the Ministry of Public Health No. 94 (1988).
Names and Schedule of Narcotics under the Narcotics Act
B.E. 2522, 1979.

E/NL.1989/36   Notification of the Ministry of Public Health No. 98 (1988).
Name and Schedule of Narcotics under the Narcotics Act.
B.E. 2522, 1979.

Philippines – E/NL.1989/37-39 (E)

E/NL.1989/37   Board Regulation No. 1 s. 1988, 18 Feburary 1988. Amending
Board Regulation No. 1 s. 1973, listing Tussionex and Mercodol
as exempt preparations.

E/NL.1989/38   Board Regulation No. 2 s. 1988, 17 March 1988. Amending Board
Regulation No. 6 s. 1972 by adding Ephedrine, Pseudoephedrine
and any of their salts as well as preparations containing any
of said drugs in the list of regulated drugs; and providing
for certain exceptions.

E/NL.1989/39   Board Regulation No. 2.A s. 1988, 17 March 1988. Amendment of
Board Regulation No. 2.A s. 1985, as amended by Board
Regulation No. 1 s. 1987, classifying Benzodiazepine
substances and certain Benzodiazepine preparations as
regulated drugs; providing for exemptions and prescribing
conditions/requirements therefor.

Chile - E/NL.1989/40-42 (S)

E/NL.1989/40   Resolución No. 2194. Advertencias en medicamentos que contienen Benzodiazepinas. 9 de marzo de 1989.

E/NL.1989/41   Decreto No. 383. Modifica decretos supremos No. 404 y 405, ambos de 1983, del Ministerio de Salud. 6 de noviembre de 1989.

E/NL.1989/42   Decreto No. 406. Modifica decretos supremos No. 404 y 405 de 1983, y 67 de 1985, todos del Ministerio de Salud. 30 de noviembre de 1989.

Chile - E/NL.1989/40-42 (E)

E/NL.1989/40   Resolution No. 2194. Warnings on medicines that contain benzodiazepines. 9 March 1989.

E/NL.1989/41   Decree No. 383. Amends Supreme Decrees No. 404 and No. 405 of 1983 of the Ministry of Health. 6 November 1989.

E/NL.1989/42   Decree No. 406. Amends Supreme Decrees No. 404 and No. 405 of 1983 and No. 67 opf 1985 of the Ministry of Health. 30 November 1989.

Ecuador - E/NL.1989/43-44 (S)

E/NL.1989/43   Acuerdo Interministerial No. 282 del 20 de mayo de 1986. Comisión Especial para que conozca, estudie y apruebe las solicitudes de importación de ácido clorhídrico y de éter etílico.

E/NL.1989/44   Acuerdo No. 476 de 5 de agosto de 1986. Ampliación del Acuerdo Interministerial No. 282.

Equateur - E/NL.1989/43-44 (F)

E/NL.1989/43   Décision interministérielle No. 282 du 20 mai 1986. Commission spéciale créée en vue de prendre connaissance, étudier et approuver les demandes d'importation d'acide chlorhydrique et d'éther éthylique.

E/NL.1989/44   Décision No. 476 du 5 août 1986. Extension de la Décision interministérielle No. 282.

Mexico - E/NL.1989/45-46 (S)

E/NL.1989/45   Decreto por el que se reforma y adiciona diversas disposiciones del Código Penal para el Distrito Federal en materia de fuero común, y para toda la República en materia de fuero federal. 1º de febrero de 1989.

E/NL.1989/46   Ley que establece, reforma, adiciona y deroga diversas disposiciones fiscales y que adiciona la Ley General de Sociedades Mercantiles. 19 de diciembre de 1989.

<u>Mexico - E/NL.1989/45-46 (E)</u>

E/NL.1989/45   Decree amending and supplementing various provisions of the
                Penal Code for ordinary offences in the Federal District and
                for federal offences throughout the Republic. 1 February 1989.

E/NL.1989/46   Act introducing, amending, supplementing and repealing various
                fiscal provisions and supplementing the General Companies
                Act. 19 December 1989.

1990

<u>Jordan - E/NL.1990/1 (E)</u>

E/NL.1990/1   Law No. 11 of 1988 on Narcotic Drugs and Psychotropic
                Substances.

<u>France - E/NL.1990/2 (F)</u>

E/NL.1990/2   Décret No. 89.880 du 6 décembre 1989. Création du Comité
                interministériel de lutte contre la drogue et de la délégation
                générale.

<u>Finland - E/NL.1990/3 (E)</u>

E/NL.1990/3   Decree No. 1119/88 concerning amendment of section 1 of the
                Narcotics Statute given at Helsinki on 23 December 1988.

<u>USSR - E/NL.1990/4-8 (E)</u>

E/NL.1990/4   Decree of the Presidium of the Supreme Soviet of the USSR of
                25 April 1974. Explanation on the procedure for the
                application of article 10.

E/NL.1990/5   List of narcotic substances and narcotic medicinal
                preparations, as of 1 January 1985.

E/NL.1990/6   Conclusion and recommendations of 14 November 1986 of the
                Permanent Committee for the Control of Narcotic Drugs under
                the Ministry of Public Health of the USSR. Definition of
                large amounts in respect of narcotic drugs detected in
                unlawful possession or traffic and definition of negligible
                amounts of narcotic substances.

E/NL.1990/7   Resolution of the Council of Ministers of the USSR of 12 June
                1987. On the prohibition of the planting and growing by
                citizens of the opium poppy. Description of poppy varieties.

E/NL.1990/8   Decree of the Presidium of the Supreme Soviet of the USSR of
                22 June 1987 (excerpt). On the introduction of amendments to
                certain legislative acts of the USSR.

<u>Cape Verde - E/NL.1990/9 (E)</u>

E/NL.1990/9   Regulation governing the commission for co-ordinating the
                fight against drugs. 12 January 1990.

Afghanistan – E/NL.1990/10 (E)

E/NL.1990/10   Decree of 20 May 1990 on the creation of a high commission for combatting the production, trafficking and use of narcotics.

Suisse – E/NL.1990/11 (F)

E/NL.1990/11   Ordonnance de l'OFSP concernant les stupéfiants et autres substances et préparations du 8 novembre 1984 (Etat le ler janvier 1990).

Sudan – E/NL.1990/12 (E)

E/NL.1990/12   Hashish and Opium Ordinance, 1924, amendment No. 1, 1989.

Perú – E/NL.1990/13 (S)

E/NL.1990/13   Resolución suprema No. 005-90-EF sobre fiscalización de productos consumos químicos.

Peru – E/NL.1990/13 (E)

E/NL.1990/13   Supreme Resolution No. 005-90-EF monitoring chemical products or inputs.

Bahamas – E/NL.1990/14-15 (E)

E/NL.1990/14   The Dangerous Drugs (Prescription of Minimum Amounts) Rules, 1989.

E/NL.1990/15   Act to amend the Dangerous Drugs Acts Act No. 3 of 1989.

Czechoslovakia – E/NL.1990/16 (E)

E/NL.1990/16   Law of 28 March 1989 on the protection against alcoholism and other toxicomania.

United Kingdom – E/NL.1990/17 (E)

E/NL.1990/17   Criminal Justice (International Co-operation) Act 1990.

España – E/NL.1990/18 (S)

E/NL.1990/18   Orden No. 23803 de 28 de septiembre de 1989, por la que se incluyen determinados principios activos en las listas III y IV anexas al Convenio de sustancias psicotrópicas de 1971.

Spain – E/NL.1990/18 (E)

E/NL.1990/18   Order No. 23,803 of 28 September 1989 requiring the inclusion of specified active principles in Schedules III and IV annexed to the 1971 Convention on Psychotropic Substances.

Hongrie – E/NL.1990/19 (F)

E/NL.1990/19   Arrêté Nº 25/1989 VIII.5. du Ministre des affaires sociales et de la santé.

Suisse - E/NL.1990/20-23 (F)

E/NL.1990/20   Code pénal suisse: Articles 58 à 60.
Peines, mesures de sûreté et autres mesures.

E/NL.1990/21   Code pénal suisse: Article 144.
Infractions contre le patrimoine: Recel.

E/NL.1990/22   Code pénal suisse: Article 305bis et 305ter.
Législation sur le blanchissage d'argent et le défaut de
vigilance en matière d'opérations financières.

E/NL.1990/23   Loi fédérale sur les banques et les caisses d'épargne:
Articles 3, 3bis et 3ter. Autorisation pour la banque
d'exercer son activité.

Sweden - E/NL.1990/24-25 (E)

E/NL.1990/24   Decree by the National Board of Health and Welfare concerning
additions to the National Board of Health and Welfare
Directions (SOSFS 1987:2) on the lists of narcotics,
SOSFS 1989:25.

E/NL.1990/25   Decree by The National Board of Health and Welfare concerning
additions to the National Board of Health and Welfare
Directions (SOSFS 1987:2) on the lists of narcotics,
SOSFS 1989:31.

Philippines - E/NL.1990/26-28 (E)

E/NL.1990/26   Board Regulation No. 5 s. 1989, 17 August 1989. Inclusion of
Buprenorphine and Pemoline; their salts and isomers, and salts
of isomers; and compounds, mixtures, and preparations
containing such substances in the list of dangerous drugs.

E/NL.1990/27   Board Regulation No. 7 s. 1989, 19 October 1989. Providing
guidelines for the implementation of Board Regulations wherein
certain provisions of the Generics Act of 1988 (R.A. 6675) are
applicable.

E/NL.1990/28   Board Regulation No. 9 s. 1989, 19 October 1989. Exempt
regulated preparations.

United States of America - E/NL.1990/29 (E)

E/NL.1990/29   Final Rule Implementing the Chemical Diversion and Trafficking
Act of 1988. Parts 1310 and 1313.

France - E/NL.1990/30-31 (F)

E/NL.1990/30   Extrait de la loi No. 89.935 du 29 décembre 1989.
Modification de l'article 64 du code des douanes.

E/NL.1990/31   Loi No. 90.614 du 12 juillet 1990 relative à la lutte contre
le blanchiment des capitaux provenant du trafic des
stupéfiants.

Suisse E/NL.1990/32 (F)

E/NL.1990/32   Loi fédérale du 20 mars 1981 sur l'entraide judiciaire internationale en matière criminelle.

Switzerland E/NL.1990/32 (E)

E/NL.1990/32   Federal Act on International Mutual Assistance in Criminal Matters (IMAC) (Act on International Criminal Assistance) of the 20th of March, 1981.

Bangladesh E/NL.1990/33 (E)

E/NL.1990/33   The Narcotics Control Act, 1990. Act No. XX of 1990.

Lebanon E/NL.1990/34-35 (E)

E/NL.1990/34   Decision No. 51/1 Concerning the Regulation of Narcotics Substances.

E/NL.1990/35   Decision No. 52/1 Concerning the Regulation of Psychotropic Substances and Schedules I to V annexed.

Afghanistan	1990/10	Hong Kong 1987/42-43, 1988/75-76, 1989/2
Argentina	1987/30-36, 1988/53-59, 1989/17	Hungary 1987/27-28, 1988/60-61, 1989/29, 1989/30, 1990/19
Australia	1988/1-2	India 1987/45, 1989/9-10,18-19
Austria	1987/37-38	Israel 1988/43
Bahamas	1988/10-12, 1990/14-15	Italy 1987/29, 1988/5-9,85
Bangladesh	1990/33	Jordan 1990/1
Belgium	1987/47-48, 1988/26-27, 1989/11, 1989/12	Lebanon 1990/34-35
		Luxembourg 1987/57-61, 1989/23
Benin	1988/18	Malaysia 1988/28-31,77-83
Bolivia	1988/25	Malta 1987/81-87
Canada	1989/3-4	Mauritius 1987/8
Cap Verde	1988/32, 1990/9	Mexico 1989/45-46
Cayman Islands	1987/44, 1988/33	Netherlands Antilles 1988/69-72
Chile	1988/50-52, 1989/40-42	New Caledonia 1989/34
China, People's Republic	1987/13	New Zealand 1988/44-45
Colombia	1987/66-71, 1988/46-48	Oman 1987/76-79
Costa Rica	1987/39, 1989/22	Pakistan 1988/49
Cyprus	1987/46	Paraguay 1987/63
Czechoslovakia	1990/16	Peru 1990/13
C/te d'Ivoire	1988/16-17	Philippines 1987/1-7, 1989/37-39, 1990/26-28
Dominica	1989/24	
Ecuador	1987/72, 1989/43-44	Polynesia, French 1987/21-23, 1989/33
Egypt	1989/14	Qatar 1987/62, 1988/84
Finland	1990/3	Romania 1988/73
France	1987/49-56,64-65, 1988/19-20, 1989/1,5-8, 1990/2,30-31	Saint Lucia 1989/13
		San Marino 1988/42
Germany, Fed. Rep.	1987/73-74	Senegal 1988/13-15
Guinea-Bissau	1987/12	Singapore 1987/40-41

Spain	1987/24-26, 1988/3-4,21-24,
	1990/18
Sri Lanka	1988/74
Sudan	1990/12
Sweden	1988/62-66, 1990/24, 1990/25
Switzerland	1990/11,20-23,32
Syrian Arab Republic	1987/88-89
Thailand	1988/35-39,67-68, 1989/15-16,
	1989/35-36
Trinidad and Tobago	1988/34
Tunisia	1987/9
Turkey	1988/40-41
Turks and Caicos Islands	1987/10-11
United Arab Emirates	1987/75
United Kingdom	1987/15-20, 1989/31-32,
	1990/17
United States of America	1987/14,
	1989/27-28, 1990/29
Uruguay	1989/20-21
USSR	1990/4-8
Venezuela	1987/80
Zambia	1989/25-26

PART III

Afghanistan

National co-ordination committee   1990/10

Argentina

Abuse of drugs by minors			1989/17
Advertisements		1989/17,	1988/53
Aggravating circumstances			1989/17
Chemical analysis of drugs/narcotics laboratories		1989/17,	1987/36
Coca leaves (chewing of)			1989/17
Commission on Narcotic Drugs	1988/59,	1988/57,	1988/55,
	1988/54,	1987/31,	1987/30
Confiscation of materials and equipment used for illicit drug production or manufacture			1989/17
Confiscation of narcotic drugs and psychotropic substances			1989/17
Confiscation of proceeds and property			1989/17
Consumption of drugs – in public places/in group/individual			1989/17
Control on licit traffic: licences, record-keeping, inspection		1989/17,	1988/58
Controlled deliveries			1989/17
Convention on psychotropic substances, 1971	1988/57,	1988/54,	1987/35,
			1987/30
Customs		1987/36,	1987/30
Destruction of drugs and substances confiscated			1989/17
Detoxification			1989/17
Disclosure of information/confidentiality, bank secrecy			1989/17
Drug abuse prevention		1987/32,	1987/31
Education/information campaigns		1989/17,	1987/32
Fraud and forgery on medical prescriptions			1989/17
Illicit cultivation-offence-penalties			1989/17
Illicit trafficking-offence-penalties		1989/17,	1987/30
Impact of treatment on prosecution, conviction or punishment			1989/17
Import certificates/export authorizations			1987/30
Import/export (prohibition/control on)	1988/58,	1987/36,	1987/35
Incitation, counselling, facilitation, promotion of drug abuse		1989/17,	1988/55
International Narcotics Control Board		1987/35,	1987/30
Manufacture, processing (prohibition/control on)		1989/17,	1988/58
Medical prescriptions (control of)	1989/17,	1988/53,	1987/34
Medical, dental, veterinary profession (regulations on)			1987/34
Money laundering-offence-penalties			1989/17
Narcotic drugs and pharmaceutical preparations containing them (Schedules)	1989/17,	1988/59,	1988/55,
		1987/36,	1987/30
National co-ordination committee			1988/56
Neglect			1989/17

Import/export (estimates of)		1987/38
Import/export (prohibition/control on)	1987/38,	1987/37
Incitation, counselling, facilitation, promotion of drug abuse		1987/37
Keeping of medical records		1987/37
Keeping of pharmaceutical records		1987/37
Manufacture, processing (prohibition/control on)		1987/38
Medical prescriptions (control of)		1987/37
Medical, dental, veterinary profession (regulations on)		1987/37
Narcotic drugs and pharmaceutical preparations containing them (Schedules)	1987/38,	1987/37
Offence committed in education establishments		1987/37
Organized criminal group		1987/37
Participation in, conspiracy to commit, attempt to commit, offence		1987/37
Penalties – fines		1987/37
Penalties – imprisonment		1987/37
Pharmaceutical profession (regulations on)	1987/38,	1987/37
Possession (control on/prohibition)		1987/37
Possession for personal consumption/for traffic		1987/37
Possession of drug-offence-penalties		1987/37
Power of entry, search, inspection		1987/37
Production (control on/prohibition)	1987/38,	1987/37
Protocol of 1972, amending the Single Convention on Narcotic Drugs, 1961		1987/37
Psychotropic substances and pharmaceutical preparations containing them (Schedules)	1987/38,	1987/37
Purchase and sale (prohibition/control on)		1987/37
Quantities and degree of danger of drugs trafficked		1987/37
Recidivism		1987/37
Registration, reporting of drug abusers		1987/37
Seizure, confiscation of means of transport used in offence (aircraft-vessel)		1987/37
Single Convention on Narcotic Drugs, 1961	1987/37,	1987/38
Storage of drugs confiscated/security measures		1987/37
Storage of drugs in pharmacies/security measures	1987/38,	1987/37
Surveillance of borders, ports and airports		1987/37
Trade and distribution (prohibition/control on)	1987/38,	1987/37
Transit/diversion (control on)		1987/37
Treatment and aftercare		1987/37
Treatment as alternative to conviction or punishment		1987/37
Victimization of minors, handicapped		1987/37

Bahamas

Aid, facilitation, counselling to commit offence	1988/11,	1988/10
Assessment of value of proceeds		1988/11
Compensation for undue seizure or confiscation		1988/11
Confiscation of materials and equipment used for illicit drug production or manufacture		1988/10
Confiscation of narcotic drugs and psychotropic substances		1988/10
Confiscation of proceeds and property	1988/11,	1988/10
Control on licit traffic: licences, record-keeping, inspection		1988/10
Cultivation of cannabis plants (control on/prohibition)		1988/10

Bangladesh

Accessory penalties	1990/33
Aid, facilitation, counselling to commit offence	1990/33
Appeal	1990/33
Chemical analysis of drugs/narcotics laboratories	1990/33
Compulsory treatment	1990/33
Confiscation of materials and equipment used for illicit drug production or manufacture	1990/33
Confiscation of narcotic drugs and psychotropic substances	1990/33
Consumption of drugs-offence-penalties	1990/33
Control on licit traffic: licences, record-keeping, inspection	1990/33
Destruction of drugs and substances confiscated	1990/33
Disposal of proceeds, property confiscated/revolving fund	1990/33
Drug abuse prevention	1990/33
Education/information campaigns	1990/33
Evidence (rules of)	1990/33
Freezing of property, restraint orders	1990/33
Illicit cultivation-offence-penalties	1990/33
Import/export (prohibition/control on)	1990/33
Internal concealment of drugs/body searches	1990/33
Investigation into banks, financial or commercial records	1990/33
Manufacture, processing (prohibition/control on)	1990/33
Materials, equipment used for illicit drug production, manufacture (control on)	1990/33
Medical prescriptions (control of)	1990/33
Medical, dental, veterinary profession (regulations on)	1990/33
Narcotic drugs and pharmaceutical preparations containing them (Schedules)	1990/33
National co-ordination committee	1990/33
Offence by corporations, companies	1990/33
Penalties – death penalty	1990/33
Penalties – fines	1990/33
Penalties – imprisonment	1990/33
Possession (control on/prohibition)	1990/33
Power of entry, search, inspection	1990/33
Power to arrest	1990/33
Power to obtain information	1990/33
Premises used for committing offence (closing of, confiscation of)	1990/33
Production (control on/prohibition)	1990/33
Providing premises to commit offence	1990/33
Psychotropic substances and pharmaceutical preparations containing them (Schedules)	1990/33
Purchase and sale (prohibition/control on)	1990/33
Quantities and degree of danger of drugs trafficked	1990/33
Quantities possessed (small/large amounts)	1990/33
Recidivism	1990/33
Registration, reporting of drug abusers	1990/33
Rehabilitation, social reintegration	1990/33
Research on drug addiction; epidemiological surveys	1990/33
Seizure, confiscation of means of transport used in offence (aircraft-vessel)	1990/33
Storage of drugs in pharmacies/security measures	1990/33
Trade and distribution (prohibition/control on)	1990/33
Transport (prohibition/control on)	1990/33
Treatment and aftercare	1990/33
Treatment centres/facilities	1990/33

Belgium

Benin

Medical prescriptions (control of)	1988/18
Narcotic drugs and pharmaceutical preparations containing them (Schedules)	1988/18
Offence committed abroad (jurisdiction on)	1988/18
Participation in, conspiracy to commit, attempt to commit, offence	1988/18
Penalties - fines	1988/18
Penalties - imprisonment	1988/18
Pharmaceutical profession (regulations on)	1988/18
Police custody	1988/18
Possession (control on/prohibition)	1988/18
Power of entry, search, inspection	1988/18
Power to arrest	1988/18
Premises used for committing offence (closing of, confiscation of)	1988/18
Production (control on/prohibition)	1988/18
Providing premises or instrumentalities for drug abuse	1988/18
Psychotropic substances and pharmaceutical preparations containing them (Schedules)	1988/18
Purchase and sale (prohibition/control on)	1988/18
Recidivism	1988/18
Special courts, military tribunals	1988/18
Trade and distribution (prohibition/control on)	1988/18
Transport (prohibition/control on)	1988/18
Treatment as alternative to conviction or punishment	1988/18
Victimization of minors, handicapped	1988/18

Bolivia

Aggravating circumstances	1988/25
Bail	1988/25
Coca leaves (chewing of)	1988/25
Commercial carriers/security measures	1988/25
Confiscation of illicitly cultivated areas	1988/25
Confiscation of materials and equipment used for illicit drug production or manufacture	1988/25
Confiscation of proceeds and property	1988/25
Consumption of drugs-offence-penalties	1988/25
Control on licit traffic: licences, record-keeping, inspection	1988/25
Cultivation of coca bush (control on/prohibition)	1988/25
Customs	1988/25
Definitions	1988/25
Early release, parole, probation	1988/25
Education/information campaigns	1988/25
Eradication of plants illicitly cultivated/substitution programmes	1988/25
Extradition	1988/25
Fraud and forgery on medical prescriptions	1988/25
Illicit trafficking-offence-penalties	1988/25
Import certificates/export authorizations	1988/25
Import/export (prohibition/control on)	1988/25
Incitation, induction to commit offence	1988/25
International co-operation	1988/25
Juvenile offenders	1988/25
Keeping of pharmaceutical records	1988/25

Bolivia (con't.)

Manufacture, processing (prohibition/control on)	1988/25
Medical prescriptions (control of)	1988/25
Medical, dental, veterinary profession (regulations on)	1988/25
Mutual legal assistance	1988/25
National co-ordination committee	1988/25
Offence by public officer/corruption of public officers	1988/25
Organized criminal group	1988/25
Participation in, conspiracy to commit, attempt to commit, offence	1988/25
Penalties – fines	1988/25
Penalties – imprisonment	1988/25
Pharmaceutical laboratories (control on)	1988/25
Pharmaceutical profession (regulations on)	1988/25
Possession (control on/prohibition)	1988/25
Premises used for committing offence (closing of, confiscation of)	1988/25
Production (control on/prohibition)	1988/25
Purchase and sale (prohibition/control on)	1988/25
Quantities and degree of danger of drugs trafficked	1988/25
Quantities possessed (small/large amounts)	1988/25
Recidivism	1988/25
Rehabilitation, social reintegration	1988/25
Storage of drugs in pharmacies/security measures	1988/25
Substances used in illicit manufacture of drugs (monitoring of)	1988/25
Trade and distribution (prohibition/control on)	1988/25
Transport (prohibition/control on)	1988/25
Treatment and aftercare	1988/25
Treatment centres/facilities	1988/25
Use of arms/violence	1988/25

Canada

Acquisition, possession, use of property derived from illicit traffic-offence-penalties		1989/3
Advertisements		1989/4
Appeal		1989/3
Burden of proof of origin of property		1989/3
Compensation for undue seizure or confiscation		1989/3
Confiscation of proceeds and property		1989/3
Consumption of drugs-offence-penalties		1989/4
Definitions	1989/4,	1989/3
Disclosure of information/confidentiality, bank secrecy		1989/3
Evidence (rules of)		1989/3
Freezing of property, restraint orders		1989/3
Illicit cultivation-offence-penalties		1989/4
Illicit trafficking-offence-penalties		1989/3
Import/export (prohibition/control on)		1989/4
Incitation, counselling, facilitation, promotion of drug abuse		1989/4
Investigation into banks, financial or commercial records		1989/3
Money laundering-offence-penalties		1989/3
Organized criminal group		1989/3
Paraphernalia (possession of)		1989/4
Participation in, conspiracy to commit, attempt to commit, offence		1989/3

Canada (con't.)

Penalties – fines	1989/3
Possession (control on/prohibition)	1989/4
Power of entry, search, inspection	1989/3
Purchase and sale (prohibition/control on)	1989/4
Rights of bona fide third parties (confiscation)	1989/3
Seizure of documents and records for investigation	1989/3
Trade and distribution (prohibition/control on)	1989/4

Cape Verde

National co-ordination committee	1990/9
Pharmaceutical profession (regulations on)	1988/32
Training of health personnel	1988/32

Cayman Islands

Aid, facilitation, counselling to commit offence		1988/33
Assessment of value of proceeds		1988/33
Boarding, searching vessel		1987/44
Compensation for undue seizure or confiscation		1988/33
Confiscation of proceeds and property		1988/33
Definitions		1988/33
Destruction of drugs and substances confiscated		1987/44
Disclosure of information/confidentiality, bank secrecy		1988/33
Disposal of proceeds, property confiscated/revolving fund		1988/33
Drug abuse prevention		1988/33
Evidence (rules of)		1987/44
Freezing of property, restraint orders		1988/33
Illicit trafficking-offence-penalties		1988/33
Import/export (prohibition/control on)		1988/33
Investigation into banks, financial or commercial records		1988/33
National advisory council on prevention and rehabilitation		1988/33
National co-ordination committee		1988/33
Participation in, conspiracy to commit, attempt to commit, offence		1988/33
Penalties – imprisonment		1988/33
Power of entry, search, inspection	1988/33,	1987/44
Power to arrest		1987/44
Power to obtain information		1988/33
Production (control on/prohibition)		1988/33
Purchase and sale (prohibition/control on)		1988/33
Research on drug addiction; epidemiological surveys		1988/33
Seizure, confiscation of means of transport used in offence (aircraft-vessel)		1987/44
Storage of drugs in pharmacies/security measures		1988/33
Trade and distribution (prohibition/control on)		1988/33

Chile

Advertisements		1989/42,	1989/40
Distribution of samples			1989/42
Narcotic drugs and pharmaceutical preparations			
containing them (Schedules)	1989/42,	1989/41,	1988/52
Packages, labels/cautions and warnings			1989/40
Psychotropic substances and pharmaceutical preparations			
containing them (Schedules)	1988/52,	1988/51,	1988/50
	1989/42,	1989/41,	1989/40

China, People's Republic

Import certificates/export authorizations	1987/13
Import/export (prohibition/control on)	1987/13
Medical prescriptions (control of)	1987/13
Packages, labels/cautions and warnings	1987/13
Pharmaceutical profession (regulations on)	1987/13
Production (control on/prohibition)	1987/13
Trade and distribution (prohibition/control on)	1987/13

Colombia

Aircraft, landing strips (control of)		1987/70,	1987/67
Armed forces			1987/66
Commercial carriers/security measures			1987/67
Confidentiality of data on drug abusers/erasing of records			1987/70
Confiscation of materials and equipment used for			
illicit drug production or manufacture			1988/47
Confiscation of narcotic drugs and psychotropic substances			1987/68
Confiscation of proceeds and property			1988/47
Control on licit traffic: licences, record-keeping,			
inspection	1988/48,	1987/71,	1987/70
Convention on psychotropic substances, 1971			1987/70
Definitions			1987/71
Disposal of proceeds, property confiscated/revolving fund		1988/47,	1987/70
Drug abuse prevention			1987/70
Early release, parole, probation			1987/68
Education/information campaigns			1987/70
Eradication of plants illicitly cultivated/substitution			
programmes			1987/66
Illicit trafficking-offence-penalties			1987/67
Import certificates/export authorizations		1987/71,	1987/70
Import/export (estimates of)			1987/70
Import/export (prohibition/control on)	1988/46,	1987/71,	1987/70
Informants (protection of, reward of, waiver of penalty for)			1987/69
Keeping of medical records			1987/70
Keeping of pharmaceutical records			1987/70
Manufacture, processing (prohibition/control on)		1988/46,	1987/70
Medical, dental, veterinary profession (regulations on)			1987/70
National co-ordination committee			1987/70
Pharmaceutical laboratories (control on)		1987/71,	1987/70

Colombia (con't.)

Possession for personal consumption/for traffic			1987/70
Power to arrest			1987/68
Preventive detention			1987/68
Production (control on/prohibition)			1987/71
Protocol of 1972, amending the Single Convention on Narcotic Drugs, 1961			1987/70
Purchase and sale (prohibition/control on)			1987/70
Registration, reporting of drug abusers			1987/70
Rehabilitation, social reintegration			1987/70
Seizure, confiscation of means of transport used in offence (aircraft-vessel)	1988/47,	1987/70,	1987/67
Single Convention on Narcotic Drugs, 1961			1987/70
Special courts, military tribunals			1987/68
Storage of drugs in pharmacies/security measures			1987/70
Substances used in illicit manufacture of drugs (monitoring of)	1987/71,	1987/70,	1987/66
Surveillance of borders, ports and airports			1987/67
Trade and distribution (prohibition/control on)	1988/46,	1987/71,	1987/70
Transport (prohibition/control on)		1988/46,	1987/71

Costa Rica

Aggravating circumstances		1989/22
Bail		1989/22
Compulsory treatment		1989/22
Confiscation of materials and equipment used for illicit drug production or manufacture	1989/22,	1987/39
Confiscation of proceeds and property		1989/22
Control on licit traffic: licences, record-keeping, inspection		1989/22
Convention on psychotropic substances, 1971		1987/39
Drug abuse prevention		1989/22
Early release, parole, probation		1989/22
Education/information campaigns		1989/22
Illicit trafficking-offence-penalties		1989/22
Import/export (prohibition/control on)		1989/22
Informants (protection of, reward of, waiver of penalty for)		1989/22
Inhalants and solvents		1989/22
International Narcotics Control Board		1987/39
Manufacture, processing (prohibition/control on)		1989/22
Materials, equipment used for illicit drug production, manufacture (control on)		1987/39
Medical prescriptions (control of)		1989/22
Money laundering-offence-penalties		1989/22
Narcotic drugs and pharmaceutical preparations containing them (Schedules)		1989/22
National co-ordination committee		1989/22
Neglect		1989/22
Offence by public officer/corruption of public officers		1989/22
Offence committed in education establishments		1989/22
Penalties - imprisonment		1989/22
Possession (control on/prohibition)		1989/22
Premises used for committing offence (closing of, confiscation of)		1989/22

Costa Rica (con't.)

Professional sanctions	1989/22
Providing premises or instrumentalities for drug abuse	1989/22
Psychotropic substances and pharmaceutical preparations containing them (Schedules)	1989/22
Rehabilitation, social reintegration	1989/22
Security measures for drug abusers	1989/22
Seizure of proceeds and property	1989/22
Seizure, confiscation of means of transport used in offence (aircraft-vessel)	1989/22
Single Convention on Narcotic Drugs, 1961	1987/39
Substances used in illicit manufacture of drugs (monitoring of)	1989/22, 1987/39
Trade and distribution (prohibition/control on)	1989/22
Treatment and aftercare	1989/22
Victimization of minors, handicapped	1989/22

Cyprus

Convention on psychotropic substances, 1971	1987/46
Narcotic drugs and pharmaceutical preparations containing them (Schedules)	1987/46
Psychotropic substances and pharmaceutical preparations containing them (Schedules)	1987/46

Czechoslovakia

Body fluid analysis to detect drug abuse	1990/16
Compulsory treatment	1990/16
Drug abuse prevention	1990/16
Education/information campaigns	1990/16
Incitation, counselling, facilitation, promotion of drug abuse	1990/16
Manufacture, processing (prohibition/control on)	1990/16
Narcotic drugs and pharmaceutical preparations containing them (Schedules)	1990/16
National advisory council on prevention and rehabilitation	1990/16
Psychotropic substances and pharmaceutical preparations containing them (Schedules)	1990/16
Purchase and sale (prohibition/control on)	1990/16
Registration, reporting of drug abusers	1990/16
Trade and distribution (prohibition/control on)	1990/16
Treatment and aftercare	1990/16
Workplace and drug abuse	1990/16

Côte d'Ivoire

Accessory penalties	1988/17
Aggravating circumstances	1988/17
Burden of proof of origin of property	1988/17
Confiscation of proceeds and property	1988/17
Driving and drug abuse	1988/17
Drug abuse prevention	1988/16

Côte d'Ivoire (con't.)

Fraud and forgery on medical prescriptions		1988/17
Illicit cultivation-offence-penalties		1988/17
Illicit trafficking-offence-penalties	1988/17,	1988/16
Import/export (prohibition/control on)		1988/17
Incitation, counselling, facilitation, promotion of drug abuse		1988/17
Manufacture, processing (prohibition/control on)		1988/17
Narcotic drugs and pharmaceutical preparations containing them (Schedules)		1988/17
National co-ordination committee		1988/16
Offence by public officer/corruption of public officers		1988/17
Offence committed abroad (jurisdiction on)		1988/17
Participation in, conspiracy to commit, attempt to commit, offence		1988/17
Penalties - fines		1988/17
Penalties - imprisonment		1988/17
Pharmaceutical profession (regulations on)		1988/17
Possession for personal consumption/for traffic		1988/17
Power of entry, search, inspection		1988/17
Preventive detention		1988/17
Production (control on/prohibition)		1988/17
Psychotropic substances and pharmaceutical preparations containing them (Schedules)		1988/17
Purchase and sale (prohibition/control on)		1988/17
Recidivism		1988/17
Trade and distribution (prohibition/control on)		1988/17
Transit/diversion (control on)		1988/17
Transport (prohibition/control on)		1988/17
Use of arms/violence		1988/17
Use of minors in trafficking		1988/17
Victimization of minors, handicapped		1988/17

Dominica

Aggravating circumstances	1989/24
Boarding, searching vessel	1989/24
Confiscation of proceeds and property	1989/24
Control on licit traffic: licences, record-keeping, inspection	1989/24
Cultivation of cannabis plants (control on/prohibition)	1989/24
Definitions	1989/24
Drug abuse prevention	1989/24
Evidence (rules of)	1989/24
Import/export (prohibition/control on)	1989/24
Incitation, induction to commit offence	1989/24
Keeping of pharmaceutical records	1989/24
Medical prescriptions (control of)	1989/24
Medical, dental, veterinary profession (regulations on)	1989/24
Money laundering-offence-penalties	1989/24
Narcotic drugs and pharmaceutical preparations containing them (Schedules)	1989/24
National advisory council on prevention and rehabilitation	1989/24
National co-ordination committee	1989/24
Neglect	1989/24

Detoxification	1987/72
Drug abuse prevention	1987/72
Early release, parole, probation	1987/72
Education/information campaigns	1987/72
Eradication of plants illicitly cultivated/substitution programmes	1987/72
Expulsion/deportation of offenders	1987/72
Extradition	1987/72
Fraud and forgery on medical prescriptions	1987/72
Hospitals	1987/72
Illicit cultivation-offence-penalties	1987/72
Illicit traffic by sea	1987/72
Import certificates/export authorizations	1987/72
Import/export (prohibition/control on)	1989/44, 1989/43, 1987/72
Incitation, counselling, facilitation, promotion of drug abuse	1987/72
International Criminal Police Organization (INTERPOL)	1987/72
International Narcotics Control Board	1987/72
International co-operation	1987/72
Keeping of medical records	1987/72
Keeping of pharmaceutical records	1987/72
Manufacture, processing (prohibition/control on)	1987/72
Medical prescriptions (control of)	1987/72
Medical, dental, veterinary profession (regulations on)	1987/72
Narcotic drugs and pharmaceutical preparations containing them (Schedules)	1987/72
National advisory council on prevention and rehabilitation	1987/72
National co-ordination committee	1987/72
Packages, labels/cautions and warnings	1987/72
Penalties - fines	1987/72
Penalties - imprisonment	1987/72
Pharmaceutical laboratories (control on)	1987/72
Pharmaceutical profession (regulations on)	1987/72
Police forces	1987/72
Possession (control on/prohibition)	1987/72
Possession of drug-offence-penalties	1987/72
Premises used for committing offence (closing of, confiscation of)	1987/72
Production (control on/prohibition)	1987/72
Professional sanctions	1987/72
Providing premises or instrumentalities for drug abuse	1987/72
Psychotropic substances and pharmaceutical preparations containing them (Schedules)	1987/72
Registration, reporting of drug abusers	1987/72
Rehabilitation, social reintegration	1987/72
Research on drug addiction; epidemiological surveys	1987/72
Samples of drugs confiscated/admissible evidence	1987/72
Security measures for drug abusers	1987/72
Seizure, confiscation of means of transport used in offence (aircraft-vessel)	1987/72
Single Convention on Narcotic Drugs, 1961	1987/72
Storage of drugs in pharmacies/security measures	1987/72
Substances used in illicit manufacture of drugs (monitoring of)	1989/44, 1989/43
Trade and distribution (prohibition/control on)	1987/72
Transmission of drugs by mails	1987/72
Victimization of minors, handicapped	1987/72
World Health Organization (WHO)	1987/72

Egypt

Hungary

Drug abuse prevention			1988/61
Import certificates/export authorizations			1987/27
Import/export (prohibition/control on)			1987/27
Narcotic drugs and pharmaceutical preparations containing them (Schedules)			1989/29
National advisory council on prevention and rehabilitation			1988/61
Production (control on/prohibition)			1987/27
Psychotropic substances and pharmaceutical preparations containing them (Schedules)	1988/60,	1987/28, 1990/19,	1987/27 1989/30
Storage of drugs in pharmacies/security measures			1987/27
Trade and distribution (prohibition/control on)			1987/27
Transit/diversion (control on)			1987/27

India

Acquisition, possession, use of property derived from illicit traffic-offence-penalties			1989/10
Aggravating circumstances			1989/10
Aid, facilitation, counselling to commit offence			1989/10
Appeal			1989/10
Bail		1989/9,	1989/10
Burden of proof of origin of property			1989/10
Chemical analysis of drugs/narcotics laboratories			1989/19
Confiscation of narcotic drugs and psychotropic substances		1989/18,	1989/10
Confiscation of proceeds and property			1989/10
Convention against Illicit Traffic, 1988			1989/10
Convention on psychotropic substances, 1971			1987/45
Customs		1989/19,	1989/9
Definitions			1989/9
Destruction of drugs and substances confiscated	1989/19,	1989/18,	1989/10
Detoxification			1989/10
Disclosure of information/confidentiality, bank secrecy			1989/10
Disposal of proceeds, property confiscated/revolving fund			1989/10
Early release, parole, probation		1989/10,	1989/9
Evidence (rules of)	1989/19,	1989/18,	1989/10
Foreign court judgements			1989/10
Freezing of property, restraint orders			1989/10
Identification, tracing of proceeds			1989/10
Illicit trafficking-offence-penalties		1989/9,	1989/10
Impact of treatment on prosecution, conviction or punishment			1989/10
Informants (protection of, reward of, waiver of penalty for)			1989/10
International co-operation			1987/45
Investigation into banks, financial or commercial records			1989/10
Manufacture, processing (prohibition/control on)			1989/10
Money laundering-offence-penalties			1989/10
Narcotic drugs and pharmaceutical preparations containing them (Schedules)	1989/19,	1989/18,	1989/10
National co-ordination committee			1987/45
Offence by public officer/corruption of public officers			1989/10
Offence committed abroad (jurisdiction on)			1989/10

Mandatory residence and other security measures for suspected traffickers		1988/6,	1988/5
Narcotic drugs and pharmaceutical preparations containing them (Schedules)			1988/85
National co-ordination committee			1988/9
Offence by public officer/corruption of public officers			1988/8
Organized criminal group	1988/9,	1988/7,	1988/6
Organizing, managing, financing illicit traffic			1988/6
Penalties - fines		1988/8,	1988/6
Penalties - imprisonment	1988/9,	1988/8,	1988/7,
		1988/6,	1988/5
Penalties - labor	1988/7,	1988/6,	1988/5
Penalties - other penalties		1988/6,	1988/9
Power to obtain information			1988/9
Preventive detention			1988/6
Professional sanctions			1988/6
Psychotropic substances and pharmaceutical preparations containing them (Schedules)			1988/85
Recidivism			1988/6
Rehabilitation, social reintegration			1987/29
Rights of bona fide third parties (confiscation)			1988/6
Seizure of documents and records for investigation			1988/6
Seizure of proceeds and property			1988/6
Treatment as alternative to conviction or punishment			1987/29
Use of arms/violence		1988/7,	1988/6

Jordan

Aggravating circumstances	1990/1
Definitions	1990/1
Foreign court judgements	1990/1
Illicit cultivation-offence-penalties	1990/1
Illicit trafficking-offence-penalties	1990/1
Import/export (prohibition/control on)	1990/1
Incitation, counselling, facilitation, promotion of drug abuse	1990/1
Involvement in international criminal activities	1990/1
Manufacture, processing (prohibition/control on)	1990/1
Narcotic drugs and pharmaceutical preparations containing them (Schedules)	1990/1
Offence by public officer/corruption of public officers	1990/1
Organized criminal group	1990/1
Penalties - death penalty	1990/1
Penalties - fines	1990/1
Penalties - imprisonment	1990/1
Penalties - labor	1990/1
Possession (control on/prohibition)	1990/1
Production (control on/prohibition)	1990/1
Providing premises or instrumentalities for drug abuse	1990/1
Psychotropic substances and pharmaceutical preparations containing them (Schedules)	1990/1
Purchase and sale (prohibition/control on)	1990/1
Recidivism	1990/1
Smuggling	1990/1
Trade and distribution (prohibition/control on)	1990/1
Transport (prohibition/control on)	1990/1
Victimization of minors, handicapped	1990/1

Lebanon

Confiscation of narcotic drugs and psychotropic substances		1990/35
Control on licit traffic: licences, record–keeping, inspection	1990/35,	1990/34
Convention on psychotropic substances, 1971		1990/34
Customs		1990/35
Destruction of drugs and substances confiscated		1990/35
Distribution of samples		1990/35
Hospitals		1990/34
Import/export (prohibition/control on)	1990/35,	1990/34
Incitation, counselling, facilitation, promotion of drug abuse		1990/34
Keeping of medical records	1990/35,	1990/34
Keeping of pharmaceutical records	1990/35,	1990/34
Manufacture, processing (prohibition/control on)		1990/35
Medical prescriptions (control of)	1990/35,	1990/34
Medical, dental, veterinary profession (regulations on)		1990/35
Narcotic drugs and pharmaceutical preparations containing them (Schedules)		1990/34
Packages, labels/cautions and warnings		1990/35
Pharmaceutical profession (regulations on)		1990/35
Possession (control on/prohibition)		1990/35
Production (control on/prohibition)		1990/35
Psychotropic substances and pharmaceutical preparations containing them (Schedules)		1990/35
Purchase and sale (prohibition/control on)		1990/35
Single Convention on Narcotic Drugs, 1961		1990/34
Trade and distribution (prohibition/control on)	1990/35,	1990/34

Luxembourg

Body fluid analysis to detect drug abuse			1989/23
Confiscation of proceeds and property			1989/23
Consumption of drugs–offence–penalties			1989/23
Financial institutions (duty of vigilance, record–keeping, reporting obligation)			1989/23
Financial institutions (regulations on, sanctions, penalties)			1989/23
Internal concealment of drugs/body searches			1989/23
Money laundering–offence–penalties			1989/23
Narcotic drugs and pharmaceutical preparations containing them (Schedules)		1989/23,	1987/61
Penalties – fines			1989/23
Penalties – imprisonment			1989/23
Premises used for committing offence (closing of, confiscation of)			1989/23
Psychotropic substances and pharmaceutical preparations containing them (Schedules)	1987/59,	1987/58,	1987/57
		1989/23,	1987/60

Malta

Appeal	1987/82,	1987/81
Burden of proof of origin of property		1987/81
Confiscation of proceeds and property		1987/81
Destruction of drugs and substances confiscated		1987/81
Evidence (rules of)		1987/81
Freezing of property, restraint orders		1987/81
Hospitals	1987/86,	1987/85
Import/export (prohibition/control on)	1987/82,	1987/81
Informants (protection of, reward of, waiver of penalty for)		1987/81
Manufacture, processing (prohibition/control on)	1987/82,	1987/81
Medical prescriptions (control of)	1987/86,	1987/85

Medical, dental, veterinary profession (regulations on)	1987/82,	1987/86,	1987/85, 1987/83

Offence committed abroad (jurisdiction on)	1987/82,	1987/81
Participation in, conspiracy to commit, attempt to commit, offence	1987/82,	1987/81
Penalties – fines	1987/82,	1987/81
Penalties – imprisonment	1987/82,	1987/81
Pharmaceutical profession (regulations on)	1987/86,	1987/85
Premises used for committing offence (closing of, confiscation of)		1987/81
Preventive detention		1987/81
Psychotropic substances and pharmaceutical preparations containing them (Schedules)	1987/87,	1987/84
Purchase and sale (prohibition/control on)	1987/82,	1987/81
Registration, reporting of drug abusers		1987/83
Rights of bona fide third parties (confiscation)		1987/81
Seizure, confiscation of means of transport used in offence (aircraft-vessel)		1987/81
Storage of drugs in pharmacies/security measures		1987/81
Trade and distribution (prohibition/control on)	1987/82,	1987/81
Witnesses		1987/81

Mauritius

Aid, facilitation, counselling to commit offence	1987/8
Bail	1987/8
Burden of proof of origin of property	1987/8
Chemical analysis of drugs/narcotics laboratories	1987/8
Compulsory treatment	1987/8
Confiscation of materials and equipment used for illicit drug production or manufacture	1987/8
Confiscation of narcotic drugs and psychotropic substances	1987/8
Confiscation of proceeds and property	1987/8
Consumption of drugs-offence-penalties	1987/8
Control on licit traffic: licences, record-keeping, inspection	1987/8
Cultivation of cannabis plants (control on/prohibition)	1987/8
Cultivation of coca bush (control on/prohibition)	1987/8
Cultivation of opium poppy (control on/prohibition)	1987/8
Definitions	1987/8
Disclosure of information/confidentiality, bank secrecy	1987/8

Mauritius (con't.)

Early release, parole, probation	1987/8
Education/information campaigns	1987/8
First-aid kits on ships and aircraft	1987/8
Fraud and forgery on import/export documents	1987/8
Freezing of property, restraint orders	1987/8
Illicit cultivation-offence-penalties	1987/8
Illicit trafficking-offence-penalties	1987/8
Import certificates/export authorizations	1987/8
Import/export (prohibition/control on)	1987/8
Keeping of medical records	1987/8
Keeping of pharmaceutical records	1987/8
Manufacture, processing (prohibition/control on)	1987/8
Medical prescriptions (control of)	1987/8
Medical, dental, veterinary profession (regulations on)	1987/8
Narcotic drugs and pharmaceutical preparations containing them (Schedules)	1987/8
Offence committed abroad (jurisdiction on)	1987/8
Packages, labels/cautions and warnings	1987/8
Paraphernalia (possession of)	1987/8
Participation in, conspiracy to commit, attempt to commit, offence	1987/8
Penalties - death penalty	1987/8
Penalties - fines	1987/8
Penalties - imprisonment	1987/8
Pharmaceutical laboratories (control on)	1987/8
Pharmaceutical profession (regulations on)	1987/8
Possession (control on/prohibition)	1987/8
Possession of drug-offence-penalties	1987/8
Power of entry, search, inspection	1987/8
Power to arrest	1987/8
Premises used for committing offence (closing of, confiscation of)	1987/8
Preparatory acts	1987/8
Psychotropic substances and pharmaceutical preparations containing them (Schedules)	1987/8
Purchase and sale (prohibition/control on)	1987/8
Recidivism	1987/8
Seizure, confiscation of means of transport used in offence (aircraft-vessel)	1987/8
Storage of drugs in pharmacies/security measures	1987/8
Trade and distribution (prohibition/control on)	1987/8
Transit/diversion (control on)	1987/8
Transmission of drugs by mails	1987/8
Transport (prohibition/control on)	1987/8
Treatment and aftercare	1987/8

Mexico

Acquisition, possession, use of property derived from illicit traffic-offence-penalties	1989/46
Aggravating circumstances	1989/45
Cultivation of cannabis plants (control on/prohibition)	1989/45
Definitions	1989/46
Financial institutions (duty of vigilance, record-keeping, reporting obligation)	1989/46

Mexico (con't.)

Illicit cultivation-offence-penalties	1989/45
Illicit trafficking-offence-penalties	1989/45
Import/export (prohibition/control on)	1989/45
Incitation, counselling, facilitation, promotion of drug abuse	1989/45
Incitation, induction to commit offence	1989/45
Money laundering-offence-penalties	1989/46
Offence by public officer/corruption of public officers 1989/45	
Offence committed in education establishments	1989/45
Offence committed in penal institutions	1989/45
Organized criminal group	1989/45
Organizing, managing, financing illicit traffic	1989/45
Participation in, conspiracy to commit, attempt to commit, offence	1989/45
Penalties - imprisonment 1989/46,	1989/45
Police custody	1989/45
Possession of drug-offence-penalties	1989/45
Production (control on/prohibition)	1989/45
Professional sanctions	1989/45
Purchase and sale (prohibition/control on)	1989/45
Trade and distribution (prohibition/control on)	1989/45
Transport (prohibition/control on)	1989/45
Victimization of minors, handicapped	1989/45

Netherlands Antilles

Control on licit traffic: licences, record-keeping, inspection	1988/69
Keeping of pharmaceutical records	1988/69
Medical prescriptions (control of)	1988/69
Medical, dental, veterinary profession (regulations on)	1988/69
Narcotic drugs and pharmaceutical preparations containing them (Schedules) 1988/72, 1988/70,	1988/69
National co-ordination committee	1988/71
Packages, labels/cautions and warnings	1988/69
Pharmaceutical profession (regulations on)	1988/69
Psychotropic substances and pharmaceutical preparations containing them (Schedules)	1988/70
Single Convention on Narcotic Drugs, 1961 1988/70,	1988/69
Storage of drugs in pharmacies/security measures	1988/69

New Caledonia

Psychotropic substances and pharmaceutical preparations containing them (Schedules)	1989/34

New Zealand

Analogues of controlled substances	1988/45
Chemical analysis of drugs/narcotics laboratories	1988/45
Evidence (rules of)	1988/44
Import/export (prohibition/control on)	1988/45
Interception of telephone communications	1988/44
Narcotic drugs and pharmaceutical preparations containing them (Schedules)	1988/45

Destruction of drugs and substances confiscated	1987/63
Detoxification	1987/63
Distribution of samples	1987/63
Drug abuse prevention	1987/63
Early release, parole, probation	1987/63
Eradication of plants illicitly cultivated/ substitution programmes	1987/63
Expulsion/deportation of offenders	1987/63
Fraud and forgery on medical prescriptions	1987/63
Freezing of property, restraint orders	1987/63
Illicit cultivation—offence—penalties	1987/63
Illicit trafficking—offence—penalties	1987/63
Import/export (prohibition/control on)	1987/63
Incitation, counselling, facilitation, promotion of drug abuse	1987/63
Informants (protection of, reward of, waiver of penalty for)	1987/63
International co-operation	1987/63
Keeping of pharmaceutical records	1987/63
Manufacture, processing (prohibition/control on)	1987/63
Medical prescriptions (control of)	1987/63
Medical, dental, veterinary profession (regulations on)	1987/63
Money laundering—offence—penalties	1987/63
Narcotic drugs and pharmaceutical preparations containing them (Schedules)	1987/63
National advisory council on prevention and rehabilitation	1987/63
National co-ordination committee	1987/63
Offence by public officer/corruption of public officers	1987/63
Offence committed in education establishments	1987/63
Offence committed in penal institutions	1987/63
Offence committed in social service facilities	1987/63
Organized criminal group	1987/63
Packages, labels/cautions and warnings	1987/63
Participation in, conspiracy to commit, attempt to commit, offence	1987/63
Penalties — fines	1987/63
Penalties — imprisonment	1987/63
Pharmaceutical laboratories (control on)	1987/63
Pharmaceutical profession (regulations on)	1987/63
Police forces	1987/63
Possession (control on/prohibition)	1987/63
Possession for personal consumption/for traffic	1987/63
Power of entry, search, inspection	1987/63
Premises used for committing offence (closing of, confiscation of)	1987/63
Preparatory acts	1987/63
Production (control on/prohibition)	1987/63
Professional sanctions	1987/63
Providing premises or instrumentalities for drug abuse	1987/63
Providing premises to commit offence	1987/63
Psychotropic substances and pharmaceutical preparations containing them (Schedules)	1987/63
Purchase and sale (prohibition/control on)	1987/63
Quantities possessed (small/large amounts)	1987/63
Recidivism	1987/63
Rehabilitation, social reintegration	1987/63
Research on drug addiction; epidemiological surveys	1987/63

Paraguay (con't.)

Samples of drugs confiscated/admissible evidence	1987/63
Security measures for drug abusers	1987/63
Seizure, confiscation of means of transport used in offence (aircraft-vessel)	1987/63
Sports and drug abuse	1987/63
Storage of drugs in pharmacies/security measures	1987/63
Substances used in illicit manufacture of drugs (monitoring of)	1987/63
Syringes and hypodermic needles (control of)	1987/63
Trade and distribution (prohibition/control on)	1987/63
Training of law enforcement personnel	1987/63
Transit/diversion (control on)	1987/63
Transport (prohibition/control on)	1987/63
Treatment and aftercare	1987/63
Use of minors in trafficking	1987/63
Victimization of minors, handicapped	1987/63
World Health Organization (WHO)	1987/63

Peru

Import/export (prohibition/control on)	1990/13
Manufacture, processing (prohibition/control on)	1990/13
Substances used in illicit manufacture of drugs (monitoring of)	1990/13
Trade and distribution (prohibition/control on)	1990/13

Philippines

Advertisements	1990/28, 1990/27, 1987/2, 1987/1
Commission on Narcotic Drugs	1990/26
Control on licit traffic: licences, record-keeping, inspection	1990/27, 1989/39, 1987/2, 1987/1
Convention on psychotropic substances, 1971	1990/28, 1989/38
Definitions	1990/28
Distribution of samples	1990/28, 1990/27, 1989/39, 1989/38, 1987/1, 1987/2
Exempted preparations	1990/28, 1990/27, 1989/39, 1987/2, 1987/1
Import certificates/export authorizations	1987/2, 1987/1
Import/export (prohibition/control on)	1987/2, 1987/1
International Narcotics Control Board	1990/28
Keeping of medical records	1989/39
Keeping of pharmaceutical records	1990/28, 1990/27, 1989/39
Manufacture, processing (prohibition/control on)	1987/1, 1987/2
Medical prescriptions (control of)	1989/39, 1987/1, 1987/2
Narcotic drugs and pharmaceutical preparations containing them (Schedules)	1990/28, 1989/37
Packages, labels/cautions and warnings	1990/27, 1987/1, 1987/2
Penalties - imprisonment	1990/28
Pharmaceutical profession (regulations on)	1990/27, 1987/1, 1987/2
Production (control on/prohibition)	1987/1, 1987/2

Philippines (con't.)

Psychotropic substances and pharmaceutical preparations
    containing them (Schedules) — 1987/3, 1987/2, 1987/1
1990/28, 1990/26, 1989/39,
1989/38, 1987/7, 1987/6,
1987/5, 1987/4

Purchase and sale (prohibition/control on) — 1989/38, 1987/1, 1987/2
Single Convention on Narcotic Drugs, 1961 — 1990/28, 1989/37
Storage of drugs in pharmacies/security measures — 1987/1, 1987/2
Trade and distribution (prohibition/control on) — 1989/38

Polynesia, French

Abuse of drugs by minors	1987/23
Inhalants and solvents	1987/23
Psychotropic substances and pharmaceutical preparations containing them (Schedules)	1989/33, 1987/22, 1987/21

Qatar

Commission on Narcotic Drugs	1988/84
Confiscation of materials and equipment used for illicit drug production or manufacture	1987/62
Confiscation of narcotic drugs and psychotropic substances	1987/62
Confiscation of proceeds and property	1987/62
Control on licit traffic: licences, record-keeping, inspection	1987/62
Convention on psychotropic substances, 1971	1988/84
Customs	1987/62
Destruction of drugs and substances confiscated	1987/62
Distribution of samples	1987/62
Eradication of plants illicitly cultivated/substitution programmes	1987/62
Foreign court judgements	1987/62
Illicit cultivation-offence-penalties	1987/62
Import/export (prohibition/control on)	1987/62
Informants (protection of, reward of, waiver of penalty for)	1987/62
Juvenile offenders	1987/62
Keeping of medical records	1987/62
Keeping of pharmaceutical records	1987/62
Manufacture, processing (prohibition/control on)	1987/62
Medical prescriptions (control of)	1987/62
Medical, dental, veterinary profession (regulations on)	1987/62
Narcotic drugs and pharmaceutical preparations containing them (Schedules)	1988/84, 1987/62
Offence by public officer/corruption of public officers	1987/62
Packages, labels/cautions and warnings	1987/62
Penalties – death penalty	1987/62
Penalties – fines	1987/62
Penalties – imprisonment	1987/62
Penalties – other penalties	1987/62
Pharmaceutical profession (regulations on)	1987/62
Possession (control on/prohibition)	1987/62
Premises used for committing offence (closing of, confiscation of)	1987/62
Production (control on/prohibition)	1987/62

Qatar (con't)

Professional sanctions	1987/62
Protocol of 1972, amending the Single Convention on Narcotic Drugs, 1961	1988/84
Psychotropic substances and pharmaceutical preparations containing them (Schedules)	1988/84, 1987/62
Purchase and sale (prohibition/control on)	1987/62
Recidivism	1987/62
Rights of bona fide third parties (confiscation)	1987/62
Seizure, confiscation of means of transport used in offence (aircraft-vessel)	1987/62
Single Convention on Narcotic Drugs, 1961	1988/84
Storage of drugs in pharmacies/security measures	1987/62
Trade and distribution (prohibition/control on)	1987/62
Transport (prohibition/control on)	1987/62
Treatment and aftercare	1987/62
Treatment as alternative to conviction or punishment	1987/62
Treatment centres/facilities	1987/62
Victimization of minors, handicapped	1987/62

Romania

Narcotic drugs and pharmaceutical preparations containing them (Schedules)	1988/73

Saint Lucia

Aid, facilitation, counselling to commit offence	1989/13
Boarding, searching vessel	1989/13
Chemical analysis of drugs/narcotics laboratories	1989/13
Confiscation of proceeds and property	1989/13
Consumption of drugs-offence-penalties	1989/13
Control on licit traffic: licences, record-keeping, inspection	1989/13
Cultivation of cannabis plants (control on/prohibition)	1989/13
Definitions	1989/13
Evidence (rules of) 1989/13	
Illicit trafficking-offence-penalties	1989/13
Import/export (prohibition/control on)	1989/13
Incitation, induction to commit offence	1989/13
Keeping of medical records	1989/13
Keeping of pharmaceutical records	1989/13
Manufacture, processing (prohibition/control on)	1989/13
Medical prescriptions (control of)	1989/13
Medical, dental, veterinary profession (regulations on)	1989/13
Money laundering-offence-penalties	1989/13
Mutual legal assistance	1989/13
Narcotic drugs and pharmaceutical preparations containing them (Schedules)	1989/13
National co-ordination committee	1989/13
Offence by corporations, companies	1989/13
Offence committed abroad (jurisdiction on)	1989/13
Offence committed in education establishments	1989/13
Opium (smoking of)	1989/13
Packages, labels/cautions and warnings	1989/13

Senegal (con't.)

Control on licit traffic: licences, record-keeping, inspection		1988/13
Illicit cultivation-offence-penalties		1988/13
Illicit trafficking-offence-penalties		1988/14
Import/export (prohibition/control on)		1988/13
Informants (protection of, reward of, waiver of penalty for)		1988/14
Manufacture, processing (prohibition/control on)		1988/13
Narcotic drugs and pharmaceutical preparations containing them (Schedules)	1988/13,	1988/14
National co-ordination committee		1988/15
Offence committed abroad (jurisdiction on)		1988/14
Organizing, managing, financing illicit traffic	1988/14,	1988/13
Participation in, conspiracy to commit, attempt to commit, offence		1988/14
Penalties - fines		1988/14
Penalties - imprisonment	1988/13,	1988/14
Penalties - other penalties		1988/14
Premises used for committing offence (closing of, confiscation of)		1988/14
Preparatory acts		1988/14
Production (control on/prohibition)		1988/13
Purchase and sale (prohibition/control on)		1988/13
Seizure, confiscation of means of transport used in offence (aircraft-vessel)		1988/14
Trade and distribution (prohibition/control on)		1988/13
Transit/diversion (control on)		1988/13
Transport (prohibition/control on)		1988/13

Singapore

Psychotropic substances and pharmaceutical preparations containing them (Schedules)	1987/41,	1987/40

Spain

Abuse of drugs by minors			1988/3
Acquisition, possession, use of property derived from illicit traffic-offence-penalties			1988/3
Adulterated substances			1988/3
Aggravating circumstances			1988/3
Assessment of value of proceeds			1988/3
Commission on Narcotic Drugs	1990/18,	1988/24,	1988/23,
		1988/21,	1987/25
Confiscation of materials and equipment used for illicit drug production or manufacture			1988/3
Confiscation of narcotic drugs and psychotropic substances			1987/26
Confiscation of proceeds and property			1988/3
Convention on psychotropic substances, 1971	1990/18,	1988/21,	1988/24,
			1987/25
Destruction of drugs and substances confiscated			1987/26
Detoxification			1988/3
Distribution of samples			1987/24
Drug abuse prevention			1988/22
Foreign court judgements			1988/3

Illicit cultivation-offence-penalties			1988/3
Illicit trafficking-offence-penalties	1988/3,	1987/26,	1987/25
Impact of treatment on prosecution, conviction or punishment			1988/3
Import/export (prohibition/control on)	1988/21,	1988/23,	1987/25
Incitation, counselling, facilitation, promotion of drug abuse			1988/3
Investigation into banks, financial or commercial records			1988/4
Keeping of pharmaceutical records			1987/24
Manufacture, processing (prohibition/control on)	1988/24, 1988/3,	1988/23, 1987/25	1988/21,
Materials, equipment used for illicit drug production, manufacture (control on)			1988/21
Medical prescriptions (control of)	1988/24,	1988/21,	1987/25, 1987/24
Medical, dental, veterinary profession (regulations on)		1987/25,	1987/24
Money laundering-offence-penalties			1988/3
Mutual legal assistance			1988/4
Narcotic drugs and pharmaceutical preparations containing them (Schedules)		1988/23,	1987/24
National co-ordination committee		1988/4,	1988/22
Offence by public officer/corruption of public officers			1988/3
Offence committed in education establishments			1988/3
Offence committed in penal institutions			1988/3
Organized criminal group		1988/4,	1988/3
Penalties - fines			1988/3
Penalties - imprisonment			1988/3
Penalties - other penalties			1988/3
Pharmaceutical laboratories (control on)	1988/24,	1988/21,	1987/25
Pharmaceutical profession (regulations on)			1987/24
Possession (control on/prohibition)		1988/23,	1987/25
Power to obtain information			1988/4
Production (control on/prohibition)			1988/23
Professional sanctions			1988/3
Psychotropic substances and pharmaceutical preparations containing them (Schedules)	1988/21, 1990/18,	1987/25, 1988/24	1987/24
Quantities and degree of danger of drugs trafficked			1988/3
Rehabilitation, social reintegration			1988/22
Research on drug addiction; epidemiological surveys			1988/22
Seizure of proceeds and property			1988/3
Single Convention on Narcotic Drugs, 1961		1988/23,	1987/24
Smuggling			1987/25
Special courts, military tribunals			1988/4
Storage of drugs confiscated/security measures			1987/26
Storage of drugs in pharmacies/security measures	1988/24,	1988/21,	1987/25
Surveillance of borders, ports and airports			1987/26
Trade and distribution (prohibition/control on)	1988/24,	1988/23,	1988/21, 1987/25
Transit/diversion (control on)			1987/25
Treatment and aftercare		1988/4,	1988/22
Treatment as alternative to conviction or punishment			1988/3
Treatment centres/facilities			1988/22
World Health Organization (WHO)		1988/21,	1987/25

Sri Lanka

Hospitals	1988/74
Narcotic drugs and pharmaceutical preparations containing them (Schedules)	1988/74
Registration, reporting of drug abusers	1988/74
Substitution/maintenance programmes for drug abusers	1988/74
Treatment centres/facilities	1988/74

Sudan

Consumption of drugs-offence-penalties	1990/12
Cultivation of cannabis plants (control on/prohibition)	1990/12
Cultivation of opium poppy (control on/prohibition)	1990/12
Expulsion/deportation of offenders	1990/12
Illicit traffic by sea	1990/12
Import/export (prohibition/control on)	1990/12
Manufacture, processing (prohibition/control on)	1990/12
Narcotic drugs and pharmaceutical preparations containing them (Schedules)	1990/12
Paraphernalia (possession of)	1990/12
Penalties - death penalty	1990/12
Penalties - fines	1990/12
Penalties - imprisonment	1990/12
Possession (control on/prohibition)	1990/12
Possession for personal consumption/for traffic	1990/12
Possession of drug-offence-penalties	1990/12
Premises used for committing offence (closing of, confiscation of)	1990/12
Production (control on/prohibition)	1990/12
Transit/diversion (control on)	1990/12

Sweden

Commission on Narcotic Drugs			1988/64
Customs			1988/65
Import/export (estimates of)			1988/63
International travelers carrying small quantities of preparations			1988/63
Intravenous drug abuse			1988/66
Medical prescriptions (control of)		1988/66,	1988/63
Narcotic drugs and pharmaceutical preparations containing them (Schedules)	1990/25,	1990/24,	1988/63, 1988/62
Psychotropic substances and pharmaceutical preparations containing them (Schedules)		1988/64,	1988/62
Storage of drugs in pharmacies/security measures			1988/65
Substitution/maintenance programmes for drug abusers			1988/66
Transport (prohibition/control on)			1988/65
Treatment and aftercare			1988/66
Treatment centres/facilities			1988/66

Switzerland

Switzerland (con't.)

Service of documents (Mutual legal assistance)		1990/32
Special courts, military tribunals		1990/32
Statute of limitations period		1990/32
Trade and distribution (prohibition/control on)		1990/11
Transfer of proceedings		1990/32
Witnesses		1990/32

Syrian Arab Republic

Import/export (prohibition/control on)		1987/88
Medical prescriptions (control of)		1987/88
Medical, dental, veterinary profession (regulations on)		1987/88
Pharmaceutical profession (regulations on)		1987/88
Professional sanctions		1987/88
Psychotropic substances and pharmaceutical preparations containing them (Schedules)	1987/89,	1987/88
Trade and distribution (prohibition/control on)		1987/88

Thailand

Advertisements			1988/39
Chemical analysis of drugs/narcotics laboratories		1989/16,	1989/15
Confiscation of narcotic drugs and psychotropic substances	1989/16,	1989/15,	1988/68
Consumption of drugs-offence-penalties		1988/68,	1988/67
Control on licit traffic: licences, record-keeping, inspection		1988/68,	1988/35
Customs			1988/37
Destruction of drugs and substances confiscated		1989/15,	1988/68
Import certificates/export authorizations		1988/37,	1988/35
Import/export (prohibition/control on)	1988/67,	1988/37,	1988/35, 1988/68
Incitation, counselling, facilitation, promotion of drug abuse			1988/68
Keeping of medical records			1988/35
Keeping of pharmaceutical records			1988/35
Manufacture, processing (prohibition/control on)			1988/67
Medical prescriptions (control of)			1988/35
Medical, dental, veterinary profession (regulations on)		1988/35,	1988/68
Narcotic drugs and pharmaceutical preparations containing them (Schedules)	1989/36,	1989/35, 1988/67,	1989/15, 1988/68
Packages, labels/cautions and warnings		1988/39,	1988/36
Penalties - fines	1988/67,	1988/35,	1988/68
Penalties - imprisonment	1988/67,	1988/35,	1988/68
Pharmaceutical profession (regulations on)			1988/35
Possession for personal consumption/for traffic			1988/67
Power of entry, search, inspection			1989/15
Production (control on/prohibition)			1988/68
Psychotropic substances and pharmaceutical preparations containing them (Schedules)	1988/36, 1988/67,	1988/35, 1988/39,	1988/68 1988/38, 1988/37

Turkey (con't.)

Penalties – death penalty	1988/41
Penalties – fines	1988/41
Penalties – imprisonment	1988/41
Possession for personal consumption/for traffic	1988/41
Purchase and sale (prohibition/control on)	1988/41
Recidivism	1988/41
Samples of drugs confiscated/admissible evidence	1988/40
Storage of drugs in pharmacies/security measures	1988/40
Transport (prohibition/control on)	1988/41
Treatment and aftercare	1988/41
Treatment centres/facilities	1988/41
Use of minors in trafficking	1988/41
Victimization of minors, handicapped	1988/41

Turks and Caicos Islands

Availability of persons in custody to give evidence		1987/10
Bilateral and regional agreements		1987/10
Disclosure of information/confidentiality, bank secrecy		1987/10
Examination of witnesses (Mutual legal assistance)		1987/10
International co-operation		1987/10
Mutual legal assistance	1987/10,	1987/11
Penalties – fines		1987/10
Penalties – imprisonment		1987/10
Power of entry, search, inspection		1987/10
Protocol of 1972, amending the Single Convention on Narcotic Drugs, 1961		1987/10
Provision of evidence (Mutual legal assistance)	1987/11,	1987/10
Requests for mutual legal assistance (contents)		1987/10
Single Convention on Narcotic Drugs, 1961		1987/10

United Arab Emirates

Accessory penalties	1987/75
Aggravating circumstances	1987/75
Aid, facilitation, counselling to commit offence	1987/75
Compulsory treatment	1987/75
Confiscation of materials and equipment used for illicit drug production or manufacture	1987/75
Confiscation of narcotic drugs and psychotropic substances	1987/75
Consumption of drugs-offence-penalties	1987/75
Control on licit traffic: licences, record-keeping, inspection	1987/75
Customs	1987/75
Destruction of drugs and substances confiscated	1987/75
Distribution of samples	1987/75
Eradication of plants illicitly cultivated/ substitution programmes	1987/75
Expulsion/deportation of offenders	1987/75
Hospitals	1987/75
Illicit cultivation-offence-penalties	1987/75
Import certificates/export authorizations	1987/75
Import/export (prohibition/control on)	1987/75

United Arab Emirates (con't.)

Incitation, counselling, facilitation, promotion of drug abuse	1987/75
Informants (protection of, reward of, waiver of penalty for)	1987/75
Keeping of pharmaceutical records	1987/75
Mandatory residence and other security measures for suspected traffickers	1987/75
Manufacture, processing (prohibition/control on)	1987/75
Medical prescriptions (control of)	1987/75
Medical, dental, veterinary profession (regulations on)	1987/75
Narcotic drugs and pharmaceutical preparations containing them (Schedules)	1987/75
Organized criminal group	1987/75
Packages, labels/cautions and warnings	1987/75
Penalties – death penalty	1987/75
Penalties – fines	1987/75
Penalties – imprisonment	1987/75
Pharmaceutical laboratories (control on)	1987/75
Pharmaceutical profession (regulations on)	1987/75
Possession (control on/prohibition)	1987/75
Premises used for committing offence (closing of, confiscation of)	1987/75
Preparatory acts	1987/75
Production (control on/prohibition)	1987/75
Professional sanctions	1987/75
Providing premises to commit offence	1987/75
Psychotropic substances and pharmaceutical preparations containing them (Schedules)	1987/75
Purchase and sale (prohibition/control on)	1987/75
Recidivism	1987/75
Security measures for drug abusers	1987/75
Seizure, confiscation of means of transport used in offence (aircraft-vessel)	1987/75
Trade and distribution (prohibition/control on)	1987/75
Treatment and aftercare	1987/75
Treatment as alternative to conviction or punishment	1987/75
Treatment centres/facilities	1987/75
Use of arms/violence	1987/75
Victimization of minors, handicapped	1987/75

United Kingdom

Assessment of value of proceeds	1990/17
Availability of persons in custody to give evidence	1990/17
Boarding, searching vessel	1990/17
Cannabis (smoking of)	1987/15
Confiscation of proceeds and property	1990/17
Control on licit traffic: licences, record-keeping, inspection	1987/15
Cultivation of cannabis plants (control on/prohibition)	1987/15
Customs	1990/17
Definitions	1990/17
Destruction of drugs and substances confiscated	1987/15
Execution of searches and seizures (Mutual legal assistance)	1990/17
Extradition	1990/17

United States of America

United States of America (con't.)

Packages, labels/cautions and warnings			1987/14
Participation in, conspiracy to commit, attempt to commit, offence			1987/14
Police custody			1989/28
Possession of drug-offence-penalties			1987/14
Psychotropic substances and pharmaceutical preparations containing them (Schedules)			1987/14
Purchase and sale (prohibition/control on)			1987/14
Seizure of proceeds and property			1987/14
Substances used in illicit manufacture of drugs (monitoring of)	1990/29,	1989/27,	1987/14
Trade and distribution (prohibition/control on)			1987/14
Transit/diversion (control on)			1987/14
Victimization of minors, handicapped			1987/14

Uruguay

Abuse of drugs by minors	1989/21
Confiscation of narcotic drugs and psychotropic substances	1989/21
Inhalants and solvents	1989/21
Medical prescriptions (control of)	1989/20
Narcotic drugs and pharmaceutical preparations containing them (Schedules)	1989/20
Penalties – fines	1989/21
Premises used for committing offence (closing of, confiscation of)	1989/21
Purchase and sale (prohibition/control on)	1989/20
Trade and distribution (prohibition/control on)	1989/20

USSR

Abuse of drugs by minors	1990/4
Body fluid analysis to detect drug abuse	1990/4
Commercial carriers/security measures	1990/8
Consumption of drugs-offence-penalties	1990/4
Cultivation of opium poppy (control on/prohibition)	1990/7
Destruction of drugs and substances confiscated	1990/7
Evidence (rules of)	1990/4
Internal concealment of drugs/body searches	1990/8
Manufacture, processing (prohibition/control on)	1990/7
Medical prescriptions (control of)	1990/4
Narcotic drugs and pharmaceutical preparations containing them (Schedules)	1990/5
Penalties – fines	1990/4
Possession for personal consumption/for traffic	1990/6
Possession of drug-offence-penalties	1990/6
Psychotropic substances and pharmaceutical preparations containing them (Schedules)	1990/5
Quantities possessed (small/large amounts)	1990/6
feature)working-operatingsys.Single Convention on Narcotic Drugs, 1961	1990/5
Transport (prohibition/control on)	1990/8
Witnesses	1990/4

Venezuela

Substances used in illicit manufacture of drugs
   (monitoring of)   1987/80

Zambia

Aid, facilitation, counselling to commit offence		1989/25
Assessment of value of proceeds		1989/25
Availability of persons in custody to give evidence		1989/25
Bail		1989/25
Compensation for undue seizure or confiscation		1989/25
Confiscation of proceeds and property	1989/26,	1989/25
Customs		1989/25
Definitions		1989/25
Destruction of drugs and substances confiscated		1989/25
Disposal of proceeds, property confiscated/revolving fund		1989/25
Drug abuse prevention		1989/26
Education/information campaigns		
Evidence (rules of)		1989/25
Examination of witnesses (Mutual legal assistance)		1989/25
Execution of searches and seizures (Mutual legal assistance)		1989/25
Identification, tracing of proceeds		1989/25
Interception of telephone communications		1989/25
Investigation into banks, financial or commercial records	1989/26,	1989/25
Money laundering–offence–penalties		1989/25
Mutual legal assistance		1989/25
National co-ordination committee		1989/26
Neglect		1989/25
Offence by corporations, companies		1989/25
Organizing, managing, financing illicit traffic		1989/25
Participation in, conspiracy to commit, attempt to commit, offence		1989/25
Penalties – fines		1989/25
Penalties – imprisonment		1989/25
Police custody		1989/25
Police forces		1989/25
Power of entry, search, inspection		1989/25
Power to obtain information	1989/26,	1989/25
Preventive detention		1989/25
Provision of evidence (Mutual legal assistance)		1989/25
Rights of bona fide third parties (confiscation)		1989/25
Seizure of proceeds and property		1989/25
Service of documents (Mutual legal assistance)		1989/25
Transfer of prisoners to their country		1989/25

PART IV

Abuse of drugs by minors

see: Argentina   Austria   Ecuador
       Paraguay   Polynesia, French   Spain
       USSR   Uruguay

Accessory penalties

see: Bangladesh   Benin   Côte d'Ivoire
       Italy   Senegal   Switzerland
       United Arab Emirates

Acquisition, possession, use of property derived from illicit traffic-offence-penalties

see: Australia   Canada   India
       Mexico   Paraguay   Spain
       Switzerland

Adulterated substances

see: Spain

Advertisements

see: Argentina   Belgium   Canada
       Chile   Paraguay   Philippines
       Thailand   Trinidad and Tobago

Aggravating circumstances

see: Argentina   Austria   Benin
       Bolivia   Costa Rica   Côte d'Ivoire
       Dominica   Ecuador   Egypt
       India   Italy   Jordan
       Mexico   Paraguay   San Marino
       Spain   Switzerland   Turkey
       United Arab Emirates

Aid, facilitation, counselling to commit offence

see: Bahamas   Bangladesh   Cayman Islands
       Egypt   France   Hong Kong
       India   Italy   Mauritius
       Paraguay   Saint Lucia   Senegal
       Turkey   United Arab Emirates   Zambia

Aircraft, landing strips (control of)

see: Colombia   Paraguay

Analogues of controlled substances

see: New Zealand

Appeal

see:	Australia	Bangladesh	Canada
	India	Malta	Switzerland

Armed forces

see:	Austria	Colombia	Paraguay

Assessment of value of proceeds

see:	Australia	Bahamas	Cayman Islands
	Hong Kong	Spain	United Kingdom
	Zambia		

Availability of persons in custody to give evidence

see:	Australia	Malaysia	Switzerland
	Turks and Caicos Islands	United Kingdom	Zambia

Bail

see:	Bolivia	Costa Rica	India
	Italy	Malaysia	Mauritius
	Zambia		

Bilateral and regional agreements

see:	Australia	Turks and Caicos Islands

Boarding, searching vessel

see:	Austria	Cayman Islands	Dominica
	France	Saint Lucia	United Kingdom

Body fluid analysis to detect drug abuse

see:	Czechoslovakia	Luxembourg	USSR

Burden of proof of origin of property

see: Australia   Canada   Côte d'Ivoire
      India   Italy   Malta
      Mauritius

Cannabis (smoking of)

see: United Kingdom

Chemical analysis of drugs/narcotics laboratories

see: Argentina   Bangladesh   Ecuador
      India   Mauritius   New Zealand
      Paraguay   Saint Lucia   Thailand
      Turkey

Coca leaves (chewing of)

see: Argentina   Bolivia

Commercial carriers/security measures

see: Bolivia   Colombia   USSR

Commission on Narcotic Drugs

see: Argentina   Belgium   Ecuador
      Oman   Philippines   Qatar
      Spain   Sweden

Compensation for undue seizure or confiscation

see: Australia   Bahamas   Canada
      Cayman Islands   Hong Kong   Switzerland
      Zambia

Compulsory treatment

see: Austria   Bangladesh   Benin
      Costa Rica   Czechoslovakia   Ecuador
      Egypt   Guinea-Bissau   Mauritius
      Paraguay   San Marino   United Arab Emirates

Confidentiality of data on drug abusers/erasing of records

see: Austria   Colombia   Egypt

Confiscation of illicitly cultivated areas

see: Bolivia   Ecuador

Confiscation of materials and equipment used for illicit drug production or manufacture

see: Argentina   Austria   Bahamas
      Bangladesh   Benin   Bolivia
      Colombia   Costa Rica   Ecuador
      Egypt   France   Guinea-Bissau
      Mauritius   Paraguay   Qatar
      Senegal   Spain   Switzerland
      United Arab Emirates

Confiscation of narcotic drugs and psychotropic substances

see: Argentina   Austria   Bahamas
      Bangladesh   Benin   Colombia
      Ecuador   Egypt   Guinea-Bissau
      India   Lebanon   Mauritius
      Paraguay   Qatar   Senegal
      Spain   Thailand   Turkey
      USA   United Arab Emirates Uruguay

Confiscation of proceeds and property

see: Argentina   Australia   Austria
      Bahamas   Bolivia   Canada
      Cayman Islands   Colombia   Costa Rica
      Côte d'Ivoire   Dominica   Egypt
      France   Hong Kong   India
      Italy   Luxembourg   Malaysia
      Malta   Mauritius   Pakistan
      Paraguay   Qatar   Saint Lucia
      Senegal   Spain   Switzerland
      Turkey   USA   United Kingdom
      Zambia

Consumption of drugs - in public places/in group/individual

see: Argentina   Turkey

Consumption of drugs—offence—penalties

see: Bangladesh   Benin   Bolivia
      Canada   Ecuador   Egypt
      Guinea-Bissau   Hong Kong   Luxembourg
      Mauritius   Paraguay   Saint Lucia
      Sudan   Thailand   Turkey
      USSR   United Arab Emirates

Control on licit traffic: licences, record-keeping, inspection

see:

Argentina	Austria	Bahamas
Bangladesh	Belgium	Benin
Bolivia	Colombia	Costa Rica
Dominica	Ecuador	Egypt
France	Germany, Fed. Rep.	Hong Kong
Lebanon	Malaysia	Mauritius
Netherlands Antilles	Oman	Paraguay
Philippines	Qatar	Saint Lucia
Senegal	Thailand	Trinidad and Tobago
Turkey	USA	United Arab Emirates
United Kingdom		

Controlled deliveries

see: Argentina

Convention against Illicit Traffic, 1988

see: India

Convention on psychotropic substances, 1971

see:

Argentina	Colombia	Costa Rica
Cyprus	India	Lebanon
Oman	Paraguay	Philippines
Qatar	Spain	

Cultivation of cannabis plants (control on/prohibition)

see:

Bahamas	Dominica	Ecuador
Mauritius	Mexico	Saint Lucia
Sudan	United Kingdom	

Cultivation of coca bush (control on/prohibition)

see:

Bahamas	Bolivia	Ecuador
Mauritius		

Cultivation of opium poppy (control on/prohibition)

see:

Bahamas	Ecuador	Mauritius
Sudan	USSR	

Customs

see:
Argentina	Austria	Belgium
Bolivia	Ecuador	Egypt
France	India	Lebanon
Paraguay	Qatar	Sweden
Switzerland	Thailand	United Arab Emirates
United Kingdom	Zambia	

Definitions

see:
Australia	Bahamas	Bolivia
Canada	Cayman Islands	Colombia
Dominica	Ecuador	Hong Kong
India	Jordan	Malaysia
Mauritius	Mexico	Pakistan
Philippines	Saint Lucia	Switzerland
USA	United Kingdom	Zambia

Destruction of drugs and substances confiscated

see:
Argentina	Bangladesh	Cayman Islands
Ecuador	Egypt	India
Lebanon	Malta	Paraguay
Qatar	Spain	Switzerland
Thailand	Turkey	USSR
United Arab Emirates	United Kingdom	Zambia

Detoxification

see:
Argentina	Austria	Benin
Ecuador	Egypt	Guinea-Bissau
India	Paraguay	Spain

Disclosure of information/confidentiality, bank secrecy

see:
Argentina	Australia	Bahamas
Canada	Cayman Islands	France
Hong Kong	India	Israel
Mauritius	Pakistan	Switzerland
Turks and Caicos Islands	USA	

Disposal of proceeds, property confiscated/revolving fund

see:
Australia	Bangladesh	Cayman Islands
Colombia	Egypt	India
Italy	Malaysia	Switzerland
USA	Zambia	

Distribution of samples

see: Chile   Egypt   Lebanon
      Paraguay   Philippines   Qatar
      Spain   United Arab Emirates

Driving and drug abuse

see: Côte d'Ivoire

Drug abuse prevention

see: Argentina   Bangladesh   Cayman Islands
      Colombia   Costa Rica   Czechoslovakia
      Côte d'Ivoire   Dominica   Ecuador
      France   Hungary   Paraguay
      Spain   Tunisia   Zambia

Early release, parole, probation

see: Austria   Bolivia   Colombia
      Costa Rica   Ecuador   Egypt
      India   Italy   Mauritius
      Paraguay   San Marino   USA

Education/information campaigns

see: Argentina   Austria   Bangladesh
      Bolivia   Colombia   Costa Rica
      Czechoslovakia   Ecuador   France
      Mauritius   Tunisia   Zambia

Eradication of plants illicitly cultivated/substitution programmes

see: Bolivia   Colombia   Ecuador
      Paraguay   Qatar   United Arab Emirates

Evidence (rules of)

see: Australia   Bahamas   Bangladesh
      Canada   Cayman Islands   Dominica
      Hong Kong   India   Italy
      Malaysia   Malta   New Zealand
      Saint Lucia   Switzerland   USSR
      Zambia

Examination of witnesses (Mutual legal assistance)

see: Australia   Switzerland
       Turks and Caicos Islands   Zambia

Execution of searches and seizures (Mutual legal assistance)

see: Australia   Malaysia   Switzerland
       United Kingdom   Zambia

Exempted preparations

see: France   Germany, Fed. Rep.   Philippines

Expulsion/deportation of offenders

see: Ecuador   Guinea-Bissau   Italy
       Paraguay   Sudan   Turkey
       United Arab Emirates

Extradition

see: Bolivia   Ecuador   Malaysia
       Switzerland   United Kingdom

Financial institutions (duty of vigilance, record-keeping, reporting obligation)

see: Australia   France   Italy
       Luxembourg   Mexico   Switzerland
       USA

Financial institutions (regulations on, sanctions, penalties)

see: Australia   France   Italy
       Luxembourg   Switzerland   USA

First-aid kits on ships and aircraft

see: Bahamas   Mauritius   United Kingdom

Foreign court judgements

see: India   Jordan   Qatar
       Spain   Switzerland

Fraud and forgery on import/export documents

see: Mauritius

Fraud and forgery on medical prescriptions

see:
Argentina	Bahamas	Belgium
Benin	Bolivia	Côte d'Ivoire
Ecuador	Paraguay	Turkey

Freezing of property, restraint orders

see:
Australia	Bahamas	Bangladesh
Canada	Cayman Islands	France
Hong Kong	India	Malta
Mauritius	Paraguay	

Hospitals

see:
Ecuador	Germany, Fed. Rep.	Lebanon
Malta	Sri Lanka	United Arab Emirates

Identification, tracing of proceeds

see:
Australia	Bahamas	Hong Kong
India	Pakistan	Zambia

Illicit cultivation—offence—penalties

see:
Argentina	Austria	Bahamas
Bangladesh	Canada	Côte d'Ivoire
Ecuador	Egypt	Guinea-Bissau
Jordan	Mauritius	Mexico
Paraguay	Qatar	Senegal
Spain	Switzerland	United Arab Emirates

Illicit traffic by sea

see:
Ecuador	France	Malaysia
Sudan	USA	United Kingdom

Illicit trafficking—offence—penalties

see:
Argentina	Bolivia	Canada
Cayman Islands	Colombia	Costa Rica
Côte d'Ivoire	India	Italy
Jordan	Malaysia	Mauritius
Mexico	Paraguay	Saint Lucia
San Marino	Senegal	Spain
Tunisia		

Impact of treatment on prosecution, conviction or punishment

see: Argentina   Egypt   India
           Spain

Import certificates/export authorizations

see:

Argentina	Bahamas	Belgium
Bolivia	China, People's Republic	Colombia
Ecuador	Hungary	Malaysia
Mauritius	Philippines	Thailand
United Arab Emirates		

Import/export (estimates of)

see: Austria   Belgium   Colombia
           Sweden

Import/export (prohibition/control on)

see:

Argentina	Austria	Bahamas
Bangladesh	Belgium	Benin
Bolivia	Canada	Cayman Islands
China, People's Republic	Colombia	Costa Rica
Côte d'Ivoire	Dominica	Ecuador
Egypt	France	Guinea-Bissau
Hungary	Jordan	Lebanon
Malaysia	Malta	Mauritius
Mexico	New Zealand	Oman
Paraguay	Peru	Philippines
United Arab Emirates	Turkey	USA

Incitation, counselling, facilitation, promotion of drug abuse

see:

Argentina	Austria	Benin
Canada	Czechoslovakia	Côte d'Ivoire
Ecuador	Egypt	France
Guinea-Bissau	Jordan	Lebanon
Mexico	Paraguay	Spain
Thailand	Turkey	United Arab Emirates

Incitation, induction to commit offence

see:

Bahamas	Benin	Bolivia
Dominica	Hong Kong	Mexico
Saint Lucia		

Informants (protection of, reward of, waiver of penalty for)

see:

Australia	Colombia	Costa Rica
India	Malaysia	Malta
Paraguay	Qatar	Senegal
Turkey	USA	United Arab Emirates

Information to foreign authorities on money laundering

see: Australia   France

Inhalants and solvents

see: Costa Rica   France   Polynesia, French
      Uruguay

Interception of telephone communications

see: Italy   Malaysia   New Zealand
      Zambia

Internal concealment of drugs/body searches

see: Bangladesh   France   Luxembourg
      USSR

International co-operation

see: Australia   Bolivia   Ecuador
      India   Paraguay   Switzerland
      Tunisia   Turks and Caicos Islands

International Criminal Police Organization (INTERPOL)

see: Ecuador   Switzerland

International Narcotics Control Board

see: Argentina   Costa Rica   Ecuador
      Philippines

International travelers carrying small quantities of preparations

see: Sweden

Intravenous drug abuse

see: Sweden

Investigation into banks, financial or commercial records

see: Australia   Bahamas   Bangladesh
      Canada   Cayman Islands   France
      Hong Kong   India   Italy
      Pakistan   Spain   USA
      Zambia

Involvement in international criminal activities

see: Jordan

Juvenile offenders

see: Bahamas   Bolivia   Qatar
            Switzerland

Keeping of medical records

see:	Austria	Bahamas	Belgium
	Colombia	Ecuador	Egypt
	France	Lebanon	Mauritius
	Philippines	Qatar	Saint Lucia
	Thailand	United Kingdom	

Keeping of pharmaceutical records

see:	Austria	Belgium	Bolivia
	Colombia	Dominica	Ecuador
	Egypt	France	Hong Kong
	Lebanon	Malaysia	Mauritius
	Netherlands Antilles	Paraguay	Philippines
	Qatar	Saint Lucia	Spain
	Thailand	United Arab Emirates	United Kingdom

Mandatory residence and other security measures for suspected traffickers

see: Italy   United Arab Emirates

Manufacture, processing (prohibition/control on)

see:	Argentina	Austria	Bahamas
	Bangladesh	Belgium	Benin
	Bolivia	Colombia	Costa Rica
	Czechoslovakia	Côte d'Ivoire	Ecuador
	Egypt	France	India
	Jordan	Lebanon	Malaysia
	Malta	Mauritius	Oman
	Paraguay	Peru	Philippines
	Qatar	Saint Lucia	Senegal
	Spain	Sudan	Switzerland
	USSR	United Arab Emirates	USA

Materials, equipment used for illicit drug production, manufacture (control on)

see:	Bangladesh	Costa Rica	Spain
	USA		

Medical, dental, veterinary profession (regulations on)

see:
Argentina	Austria	Bahamas
Bangladesh	Belgium	Bolivia
Colombia	Dominica	Ecuador
Germany, Fed. Rep.	Hong Kong	Lebanon
Malaysia	Malta	Mauritius
Netherlands Antilles	Paraguay	Qatar
Saint Lucia	Spain	Syrian Arab Republic
Thailand	Turkey	United Arab Emirates
United Kingdom		

Medical prescriptions (control of)

see:
Argentina	Austria	Bahamas
Bangladesh	Belgium	Benin
Bolivia	China, People's Republic	Costa Rica
Dominica	Ecuador	France
Germany, Fed. Rep.	Guinea-Bissau	Hong Kong
Lebanon	Malaysia	Malta
Mauritius	Netherlands Antilles	Oman
Paraguay	Philippines	Qatar
Saint Lucia	Spain	Sweden
Syrian Arab Republic	Thailand	USA
Uruguay	United Arab Emirates	United Kingdom

Money laundering—offence—penalties

see:
Argentina	Australia	Bahamas
Canada	Costa Rica	Dominica
France	India	Luxembourg
Malaysia	Mexico	Paraguay
Saint Lucia	Spain	Switzerland
USA	United Kingdom	Zambia

Mutual legal assistance

see:
Australia	Bahamas	Bolivia
Malaysia	Saint Lucia	Spain
Switzerland	Turks and Caicos Islands	United Kingdom
Zambia		

Narcotic drugs and pharmaceutical preparations containing them (Schedules)

see:
Argentina	Austria	Bahamas
Bangladesh	Belgium	Benin
Chile	Costa Rica	Cyprus
Czechoslovakia	Côte d'Ivoire	Dominica
Ecuador	Egypt	Finland
France	Germany, Fed. Rep.	Guinea-Bissau
Hong Kong	Hungary	India
Italy	Jordan	Lebanon
Luxembourg	Malaysia	Mauritius
Netherlands Antilles	New Zealand	Paraguay
United Arab Emirates	United Kingdom	Uruguay

National advisory council on prevention and rehabilitation

see: | Cayman Islands | Czechoslovakia | Dominica |
| Ecuador | Hungary | Paraguay |

National co-ordination committee

see: | Afghanistan | Argentina | Bangladesh |
Bolivia	Cape Verde	Cayman Islands
Colombia	Costa Rica	Côte d'Ivoire
Dominica	Ecuador	France
India	Israel	Italy
Netherlands Antilles	Paraguay	Saint Lucia
Senegal	Spain	Tunisia
Zambia		

Neglect

see: | Argentina | Bahamas | Costa Rica |
| Dominica | Guinea-Bissau | Switzerland |
| Zambia | | |

Offence by corporations, companies

see: | Argentina | Australia | Bangladesh |
| Dominica | Saint Lucia | Zambia |

Offence by public officer/corruption of public officers

see: | Argentina | Australia | Bolivia |
Costa Rica	Côte d'Ivoire	Egypt
India	Italy	Jordan
Malaysia	Mexico	Paraguay
Qatar	Spain	Turkey

Offence committed abroad (jurisdiction on)

see: | Australia | Benin | Côte d'Ivoire |
Dominica	Guinea-Bissau	India
Malta	Mauritius	Saint Lucia
Senegal	Switzerland	

Offence committed in education establishments

see: | Argentina | Austria | Costa Rica |
| Dominica | Egypt | Mexico |
| Paraguay | Saint Lucia | Spain |

Offence committed in penal institutions

see: Dominica   Egypt   Mexico
      Paraguay   Spain

Offence committed in social service facilities

see: Paraguay

Opium (smoking of)

see: Bahamas   Dominica   Saint Lucia

Organized criminal group

see: Argentina   Austria   Bolivia
      Canada   Egypt   Italy
      Jordan   Mexico   Paraguay
      Spain   Turkey   United Arab Emirates

Organizing, managing, financing illicit traffic

see: Argentina   India   Italy
      Mexico   Senegal   Zambia

Packages, labels/cautions and warnings

see: Argentina   Belgium   Chile
      China, People's Republic   Dominica   Ecuador
      France   Germany, Fed. Rep.   Lebanon
      Malaysia   Mauritius   Netherlands Antilles
      Paraguay   Philippines   Qatar
      Saint Lucia   Thailand   Trinidad and Tobago
      USA   United Arab Emirates   United Kingdom

Paraphernalia (possession of)

see: Bahamas   Canada   Dominica
      Mauritius   New Zealand   Saint Lucia
      Sudan   Turkey

Participation in, conspiracy to commit, attempt to commit, offence

see: Austria   Bahamas   Benin
      Bolivia   Canada   Cayman Islands
      Côte d'Ivoire   Dominica   France
      Guinea-Bissau   Hong Kong   India
      Malaysia   Malta   Mauritius
      Mexico   Paraguay   Saint Lucia
      Senegal   Turkey   USA
      Zambia

Penalties – death penalty

see:
Bangladesh	Egypt	Guinea-Bissau
India	Jordan	Mauritius
Qatar	Sudan	Turkey
United Arab Emirates		

Penalties – fines

see:
Argentina	Australia	Austria
Bahamas	Bangladesh	Benin
Bolivia	Canada	Côte d'Ivoire
Dominica	Ecuador	Egypt
France	Hong Kong	India
Italy	Jordan	Luxembourg
Malaysia	Malta	Mauritius
Paraguay	Qatar	Senegal
Spain	Sudan	Switzerland
Thailand	Turkey	Turks & Caicos Islands
Uruguay	Zambia	United Kingdom

Penalties – imprisonment

see:
Argentina	Australia	Austria
Bahamas	Bangladesh	Benin
Bolivia	Cayman Islands	Costa Rica
Côte d'Ivoire	Dominica	Ecuador
Egypt	France	Hong Kong
India	Italy	Jordan
Luxembourg	Malaysia	Malta
Mauritius	Mexico	Paraguay
Philippines	Qatar	Saint Lucia
San Marino	Senegal	Spain
United Kingdom	Zambia	United Arab Emirates

Penalties – labor

see:
Egypt	Guinea-Bissau	Italy
Jordan		

Penalties – other penalties

see:
France	Italy	Malaysia
Qatar	Senegal	Spain

Pharmaceutical laboratories (control on)

see:
Argentina	Belgium	Bolivia
Colombia	Ecuador	Mauritius
Paraguay	Spain	United Arab Emirates

Pharmaceutical profession (regulations on)

see:
Argentina	Austria	Belgium
Benin	Bolivia	Cape Verde
China, People's Republic	Côte d'Ivoire	Dominica
Ecuador	France	Germany, Fed. Rep.
Hong Kong	Lebanon	Malta
Mauritius	Netherlands Antilles	Oman
Paraguay	Philippines	Qatar
Spain	Syrian Arab Republic	Thailand
United Arab Emirates		

Police custody

see:
Benin	Mexico	USA
Zambia		

Police forces

see:
Ecuador	India	Paraguay
Switzerland	Zambia	

Poppy straw (control on)

see:
India	Switzerland	United Kingdom

Possession (control on/prohibition)

see:
Austria	Bahamas	Bangladesh
Benin	Bolivia	Canada
Costa Rica	Dominica	Ecuador
Egypt	Jordan	Lebanon
Malaysia	Mauritius	Paraguay
Qatar	Saint Lucia	Spain
Sudan	United Arab Emirates	United Kingdom

Possession for personal consumption/for traffic

see:
Argentina	Austria	Bahamas
Colombia	Côte d'Ivoire	Dominica
Egypt	Guinea-Bissau	Paraguay
Saint Lucia	San Marino	Sudan
Thailand	Turkey	USSR

Possession of drug-offence-penalties

see:
Argentina	Australia	Austria
Bahamas	Dominica	Ecuador
Malaysia	Mauritius	Mexico
San Marino	Sudan	USA
USSR		

Power of entry, search, inspection

see:

Australia	Austria	Bahamas
Bangladesh	Benin	Canada
Cayman Islands	Côte d'Ivoire	Dominica
Egypt	France	Hong Kong
Malaysia	Mauritius	Paraguay
Saint Lucia	Switzerland	Thailand
Turks and Caicos Islands	Zambia	

Power to arrest

see:

Australia	Bahamas	Bangladesh
Benin	Cayman Islands	Colombia
Dominica	India	Malaysia
Mauritius	Saint Lucia	Switzerland

Power to obtain information

see:

Australia	Bahamas	Bangladesh
Cayman Islands	Dominica	Hong Kong
Israel	Italy	Malaysia
Saint Lucia	Spain	Zambia

Premises used for committing offence (closing of, confiscation of)

see:

Argentina	Bahamas	Bangladesh
Benin	Bolivia	Costa Rica
Dominica	Ecuador	Egypt
France	Guinea-Bissau	Luxembourg
Malaysia	Malta	Mauritius
Paraguay	Qatar	Saint Lucia
Senegal	Sudan	United Arab Emirates
United Kingdom	Uruguay	

Preparatory acts

see:

Bahamas	Mauritius	Paraguay
Senegal	United Arab Emirates	

Preventive detention

see:

Colombia	Côte d'Ivoire	France
India	Italy	Malaysia
Malta	Switzerland	Zambia

Production (control on/prohibition)

see:
Argentina	Australia	Austria
Bangladesh	Benin	Bolivia
Cayman Islands	China, People's Republic	Colombia
Côte d'Ivoire	Dominica	Ecuador
Egypt	France	Guinea-Bissau
Hungary	India	Jordan
Lebanon	Mexico	Paraguay
Philippines	Qatar	Saint Lucia
San Marino	Senegal	Spain
Sudan	Switzerland	Thailand
United Arab Emirates	United Kingdom	

Professional sanctions

see:
Argentina	Belgium	Costa Rica
Dominica	Ecuador	France
Italy	Mexico	Paraguay
Qatar	Spain	Syrian Arab Republic
United Arab Emirates		

Protocol of 1972, amending the Single Convention on Narcotic Drugs, 1961

see:
Argentina	Austria	Belgium
Colombia	India	Qatar
Turks and Caicos Islands		

Providing premises or instrumentalities for drug abuse

see:
Benin	Costa Rica	Ecuador
Jordan	Paraguay	

Providing premises to commit offence

see:
Argentina	Bangladesh	Dominica
Egypt	Paraguay	United Arab Emirates

Provision of evidence (Mutual legal assistance)

see:
Australia	Malaysia	Switzerland
Turks and Caicos Islands	United Kingdom	Zambia

Psychotropic substances and pharmaceutical preparations containing them (Schedules)

see:
Argentina	Austria	Bahamas
Bangladesh	Belgium	Benin
Chile	Costa Rica	Cyprus
Czechoslovakia	Côte d'Ivoire	Dominica
Ecuador	Egypt	France
Germany, Fed. Rep.	Hungary	India
Italy	Jordan	Lebanon
Luxembourg	Malaysia	Malta
Mauritius	Netherlands Antilles	New Caledonia
New Zealand	Oman	Paraguay
United Kingdom	USSR	United Arab Emirates

Purchase and sale (prohibition/control on)

see:
Argentina	Austria	Bahamas
Bangladesh	Belgium	Benin
Bolivia	Canada	Cayman Islands
Colombia	Czechoslovakia	Côte d'Ivoire
Dominica	Egypt	France
Guinea-Bissau	Hong Kong	India
Jordan	Lebanon	Malaysia
Malta	Mauritius	Mexico
Oman	Paraguay	Philippines
Qatar	Saint Lucia	San Marino
United Arab Emirates	Uruguay	USA

Quantities and degree of danger of drugs trafficked

see:
Australia	Austria	Bahamas
Bangladesh	Bolivia	Egypt
India	Malaysia	Spain
Thailand		

Quantities possessed (small/large amounts)

see:
Bahamas	Bangladesh	Bolivia
Dominica	Egypt	Malaysia
Paraguay	Saint Lucia	USSR

Recidivism

see:
Austria	Bangladesh	Benin
Bolivia	Côte d'Ivoire	Egypt
Guinea-Bissau	India	Italy
Jordan	Mauritius	Paraguay
Qatar	Turkey	United Arab Emirates

Registration, reporting of drug abusers

see: Austria   Bangladesh   Colombia

see:	Austria	Bangladesh	Colombia
	Czechoslovakia	Ecuador	Egypt
	Malta	Saint Lucia	Sri Lanka

Rehabilitation, social reintegration

see:	Argentina	Bangladesh	Bolivia
	Colombia	Costa Rica	Ecuador
	Hong Kong	Italy	Paraguay
	Spain	Switzerland	

Request for confiscation from foreign country

see:	Australia	Bahamas	Hong Kong
	Switzerland	United Kingdom	

Requests for mutual legal assistance (contents)

see:	Australia	Switzerland	Turks & Caicos Islands

Research on drug addiction; epidemiological surveys

see:	Bangladesh	Cayman Islands	Dominica
	Ecuador	France	Paraguay
	Spain	Tunisia	

Rights of bona fide third parties (confiscation)

see:	Argentina	Australia	Canada
	Egypt	India	Italy
	Malta	Qatar	Switzerland
	Zambia		

Samples of drugs confiscated/admissible evidence

see:	Argentina	Ecuador	India
	Paraguay	Thailand	Turkey

Security measures for drug abusers

see:	Costa Rica	Ecuador	Paraguay
	United Arab Emirates		

Seizure of documents and records for investigation

see:	Australia	Bahamas	Canada
	Dominica	France	Hong Kong
	Italy	Saint Lucia	Switzerland

Seizure of proceeds and property

see:
Costa Rica	France	Hong Kong
India	Italy	Malaysia
Spain	USA	United Kingdom
Zambia		

Seizure, confiscation of means of transport used in offence (aircraft-vessel)

see:
Argentina	Austria	Bahamas
Bangladesh	Cayman Islands	Colombia
Costa Rica	Dominica	Ecuador
Egypt	Malaysia	Malta
Mauritius	Paraguay	Qatar
Saint Lucia	Senegal	Switzerland
United Arab Emirates		

Service of documents (Mutual legal assistance)

see:
Australia	Malaysia	Saint Lucia
Switzerland	United Kingdom	Zambia

Single Convention on Narcotic Drugs, 1961

see:
Argentina	Austria	Belgium
Colombia	Costa Rica	Ecuador
France	India	Lebanon
Netherlands Antilles	Philippines	Qatar
Saint Lucia	Spain	Turks & Caicos Islands
USSR		

Smuggling

see:
Bahamas	Jordan	Spain

Special courts, military tribunals

see:
Benin	Colombia	India
Spain	Switzerland	

Sports and drug abuse

see:
Argentina	Paraguay

Statute of limitations period

see:
Egypt	Switzerland

Storage of drugs confiscated/security measures

see: Austria   India   Spain
      Thailand

Storage of drugs in pharmacies/security measures

see: Argentina   Austria   Bahamas
      Bangladesh   Belgium   Bolivia
      Cayman Islands   Colombia   Dominica
      Ecuador   France   Germany, Fed. Rep.
      Guinea-Bissau   Hungary   Malaysia
      Malta   Mauritius   Netherlands Antilles
      Oman   Paraguay   Philippines
      Qatar   Saint Lucia   Spain
      Sweden   Turkey   United Kingdom

Substances used in illicit manufacture of drugs (monitoring of)

see: Argentina   Belgium   Bolivia
      Colombia   Costa Rica   Ecuador
      Paraguay   Peru   Thailand
      USA   United Kingdom   Venezuela

Substitution/maintenance programmes for drug abusers

see: Sri Lanka   Sweden   Thailand

Surveillance of borders, ports and airports

see: Austria   Colombia   India
      Spain

Syringes and hypodermic needles (control of)

see: France   New Zealand   Paraguay

Trade and distribution (prohibition/control on)

see: Argentina   Austria   Bahamas
      Bangladesh   Belgium   Benin
      Bolivia   Canada   Cayman Islands
      China, People's Republic Colombia   Costa Rica
      Czechoslovakia   Côte d'Ivoire   Dominica
      Ecuador   Egypt   France
      Germany, Fed. Rep.   Hungary   India
      Jordan   Lebanon   Malaysia
      Malta   Mauritius   Mexico
      New Zealand   Oman   Paraguay
      Uruguay   United Arab Emirates   United Kingdom

Training of health personnel

see: Cape Verde   France

Training of law enforcement personnel

see: Paraguay

Transfer of prisoners to their country

see: Malaysia   United Kingdom   Zambia

Transfer of proceedings

see: Switzerland

Transit/diversion (control on)

see: Argentina   Austria   Bahamas
      Belgium   Côte d'Ivoire   Guinea-Bissau
      Hungary   Malaysia   Mauritius
      Paraguay   Senegal   Spain
      Sudan   USA

Transmission of drugs by mails

see: Bahamas   Belgium   Ecuador
      Mauritius

Transport (prohibition/control on)

see: Bangladesh   Belgium   Benin
      Bolivia   Colombia   Côte d'Ivoire
      Dominica   Egypt   France
      Guinea-Bissau   Jordan   Mauritius
      Mexico   Paraguay   Qatar
      Saint Lucia   Senegal   Sweden
      Turkey   USSR

Treatment and aftercare

see: Argentina   Austria   Bangladesh
      Bolivia   Costa Rica   Czechoslovakia
      Dominica   Egypt   France
      Hong Kong   Mauritius   Paraguay
      Qatar   Spain   Sweden
      Turkey   United Arab Emirates

Treatment as alternative to conviction or punishment

see:
Argentina	Austria	Benin
Egypt	India	Italy
Qatar	Spain	United Arab Emirates

Treatment centres/facilities

see:
Bangladesh	Bolivia	Egypt
Qatar	Spain	Sri Lanka
Sweden	Thailand	Turkey
United Arab Emirates		

Use of arms/violence

see:
Bolivia	Côte d'Ivoire	Egypt
Italy	United Arab Emirates	

Use of minors in trafficking

see:
Côte d'Ivoire	Egypt	Paraguay
Turkey		

Victimization of minors, handicapped

see:
Austria	Benin	Costa Rica
Côte d'Ivoire	Dominica	Ecuador
Egypt	France	Jordan
Mexico	Paraguay	Qatar
Saint Lucia	San Marino	Turkey
USA	United Arab Emirates	

Witnesses

see:
Australia	Malaysia	Malta
Switzerland	USSR	

Workplace and drug abuse

see: Czechoslovakia

World Health Organization (WHO)

see:
Argentina	Ecuador	Paraguay
Spain		

PART V

A. DRUG ABUSE PREVENTION AND TREATMENT

Patterns of abuse

Abuse of drugs by minors
Intravenous drug abuse
Workplace and drug abuse
Driving and drug abuse
Sports and drug abuse
Research on drug addiction; epidemiological surveys

Prevention

Drug abuse prevention
Education/information campaigns
National advisory council on prevention and rehabilitation

Treatment

Treatment and aftercare
Substitution/maintenance programmes for drug abusers
Detoxification
Security measures for drug abusers
Rehabilitation, social reintegration
Treatment as alternative to conviction or punishment
Impact of treatment on prosecution, conviction or punishment
Compulsory treatment
Registration, reporting of drug abusers
Confidentiality of data on drug abusers/erasing of records
Treatment centres/facilities
Hospitals
Training of health personnel

B. CONTROL MEASURES ON DEMAND, SUPPLY AND TRAFFIC

Controlled substances

Narcotic drugs and pharmaceutical preparations containing them (Schedules)
Psychotropic substances and pharmaceutical preparations containing them
    (Schedules)
Substances used in illicit manufacture of drugs (monitoring of)
Inhalants and solvents
Analogues of controlled substances
Adulterated substances
Exempted preparations
Poppy straw (control on)
Cannabis (smoking of)
Coca leaves (chewing of)
Opium (smoking of)

Medical, pharmaceutical professions

Medical, dental, veterinary profession (regulations on)
Medical prescriptions (control of)
Fraud and forgery on medical prescriptions
Keeping of medical records
Hospitals
Pharmaceutical profession (regulations on)
Pharmaceutical laboratories (control on)
Advertisements
Packages, labels/cautions and warnings
Distribution of samples
Syringes and hypodermic needles (control of)
Keeping of pharmaceutical records
Storage of drugs in pharmacies/security measures

Cultivation

Cultivation of cannabis plants (control on/prohibition)
Cultivation of coca bush (control on/prohibition)
Cultivation of opium poppy (control on/prohibition)
Confiscation of illicitly cultivated areas
Eradication of plants illicitly cultivated/substitution programmes

Manufacture, production

Manufacture, processing (prohibition/control on)
Production (control on/prohibition)
Materials, equipment used for illicit drug production, manufacture (control on)

Consumption, possession

Consumption of drugs — in public places/in group/individual
Registration, reporting of drug abusers
Confidentiality of data on drug abusers/erasing of records
Possession (control on/prohibition)
Paraphernalia (possession of)
Syringes and hypodermic needles (control of)

Trade, transport, international movements

Control on licit traffic: licences, record-keeping, inspection
Purchase and sale (prohibition/control on)
Trade and distribution (prohibition/control on)
Transport (prohibition/control on)
Transit/diversion (control on)
Commercial carriers/security measures
Import/export (prohibition/control on)
Import certificates/export authorizations
Import/export (estimates of)
Fraud and forgery on import/export documents
International travelers carrying small quantities of preparations
First-aid kits on ships and aircraft
Aircraft, landing strips (control of)
Surveillance of borders, ports and airports
Customs
Transmission of drugs by mails
Seizure, confiscation of means of transport used in offence (aircraft-vessel)

C. PENAL AND RELATED PROVISIONS

Offences and offenders

Consumption of drugs-offence-penalties
Consumption of drugs - in public places/in group/individual
Fraud and forgery on medical prescriptions
Possession of drug-offence-penalties
Possession for personal consumption/for traffic
Quantities possessed (small/large amounts)
Illicit cultivation-offence-penalties
Illicit trafficking-offence-penalties
Illicit traffic by sea
Quantities and degree of danger of drugs trafficked
Smuggling
Fraud and forgery on import/export documents
Organizing, managing, financing illicit traffic
Acquisition, possession, use of property derived from illicit
    traffic-offence-penalties
Boarding, searching vessel
Money laundering-offence-penalties
Offence by corporations, companies
Neglect
Juvenile offenders

Ancillary offences

Incitation, counselling, facilitation, promotion of drug abuse
Providing premises or instrumentalities for drug abuse
Participation in, conspiracy to commit, attempt to commit, offence
Preparatory acts
Incitation, induction to commit offence
Aid, facilitation, counselling to commit offence
Providing premises to commit offence
Premises used for committing offence (closing of, confiscation of)

Aggravating circumstances

Aggravating circumstances
Use of minors in trafficking
Victimization of minors, handicapped
Use of arms/violence
Offence committed in education establishments
Offence committed in social service facilities
Offence committed in penal institutions
Offence by public officer/corruption of public officers
Organized criminal group
Involvement in international criminal activities
Recidivism

Sanctions and penalties

Penalties - imprisonment
Penalties - fines
Penalties - labor
Penalties - death penalty
Penalties - other penalties
Accessory penalties
Professional sanctions
Mandatory residence and other security measures for suspected traffickers
Security measures for drug abusers
Expulsion/deportation of offenders
Extradition
Financial institutions (regulations on, sanctions, penalties)
Premises used for committing offence (closing of, confiscation of)
Seizure, confiscation of means of transport used in offence (aircraft-vessel)

Confiscation of drugs, substances, equipment

Confiscation of narcotic drugs and psychotropic substances
Confiscation of materials and equipment used for illicit drug production or
    manufacture
Chemical analysis of drugs/narcotics laboratories
Confiscation of illicitly cultivated areas
Samples of drugs confiscated/admissible evidence
Storage of drugs confiscated/security measures
Destruction of drugs and substances confiscated

Money laundering, investigation, confiscation of proceeds

Money laundering-offence-penalties
Identification, tracing of proceeds
Investigation into banks, financial or commercial records
Financial institutions (duty of vigilance, record-keeping, reporting
    obligation)
Disclosure of information/confidentiality, bank secrecy
Financial institutions (regulations on, sanctions, penalties)
Freezing of property, restraint orders
Seizure of proceeds and property
Confiscation of proceeds and property
Assessment of value of proceeds
Burden of proof of origin of property
Disposal of proceeds, property confiscated/revolving fund
Rights of bona fide third parties (confiscation)
Compensation for undue seizure or confiscation
Offence by corporations, companies
Neglect
Information to foreign authorities on money laundering
Request for confiscation from foreign country

Investigation powers

Internal concealment of drugs/body searches
Body fluid analysis to detect drug abuse
Informants (protection of, reward of, waiver of penalty for)
Power to obtain information
Interception of telephone communications
Seizure of documents and records for investigation
Controlled deliveries
Power of entry, search, inspection
Power to arrest
Preventive detention
Police custody

Evidence

Evidence (rules of)
Witnesses
Body fluid analysis to detect drug abuse
Chemical analysis of drugs/narcotics laboratories
Samples of drugs confiscated/admissible evidence

Procedure

Bail
Early release, parole, probation
Statute of limitations period
Appeal
Offence committed abroad (jurisdiction on)
Foreign court judgements
Special courts, military tribunals
Juvenile offenders

Law enforcement personnel

Police forces
Armed forces
Training of law enforcement personnel

D.   INTERNATIONAL CO-OPERATION

Treaties and agreements

Bilateral and regional agreements
Single Convention on Narcotic Drugs, 1961
Protocol of 1972, amending the Single Convention on Narcotic Drugs, 1961
Convention on psychotropic substances, 1971
Convention against Illicit Traffic, 1988

International organizations

Commission on Narcotic Drugs
International Narcotics Control Board
World Health Organization
International Criminal Police Organization

Mutual legal assistance

International co-operation
Mutual legal assistance
Service of documents (Mutual legal assistance)
Provision of evidence (Mutual legal assistance)
Examination of witnesses (Mutual legal assistance)
Execution of searches and seizures (Mutual legal assistance)
Availability of persons in custody to give evidence
Information to foreign authorities on money laundering
Requests for mutual legal assistance (contents)
Request for confiscation from foreign country
Transfer of proceedings
Transfer of prisoners to their country

Miscellaneous

Definitions
National co-ordination committee